101 THINGS TO DO IN MILWAUKEE PARKS

A guide to the green spaces in Milwaukee

BARBARA ALI

DEDICATION

To my family, who make every day an adventure.

CONTENTS

Introduction.

My husband, and I have traveled to many countries on 6 different continents, and we always try outdoor activities in every place we visit. Even though I enjoy travel, I love coming back home to Milwaukee. As a seasoned traveler, I realize that this region has one of the best and most beautiful park systems in the world. It's no wonder we have a Gold Medal Parks program.

Our park system has long been a source of pride for Milwaukee, with its more than 140 county parks and parkways, and dozens more when you add city and village playgrounds, ball fields, and parks. We even have a park designed by Frederick Law Olmsted, the same man who designed Central Park in New York City. Actually, by the time Mr. Olmsted came to Milwaukee, he'd created the concept of park systems. For Milwaukee, he designed a 3-park system made up of Lake, Riverside, and Washington Parks. By creating a collection, each could have a different landscape. There are still trees in place today that he planted.

Creating our parks system was no minor undertaking. The park system began with the creation of the Milwaukee County Park Commission in 1907. These early commissioners selected land for natural beauty and interest, as well as various forms of recreation. They had the foresight to form a green belt with a series of scenic drives encircling the county, and added more in outlying areas for the growing population. I'm sure that if the original park commission members were still around today, they'd be so proud and excited that we are still adding new parks. The latest additions, added in 2013, were the Rotary Centennial Arboretum and Three Bridges Park.

It's impossible to cover every aspect of every park, although I'd love to do that. It's better that you get out and try something in a variety of parks and do some exploring on your own. If you need maps for any of the county parks, you can go to www.county.gov/parks and select the park system maps. There is a large poster size printed version available at most of the golf course clubhouses. I remember the first time I saw it, I was amazed at the sheer number and made it my goal to check out all of them. I still have not succeeded!

This book is a compilation of all the fun activities I've observed and tried while enjoying the parks with my friends and family. As I joined them in outings to area parks, I realized that there is much more here than just playgrounds and picnic areas. I started writing a blog in 2012, about Milwaukee area parks, www.milwaukeeparks.blogspot.com and was surprised by how much there was to do in the area. The best part is that most activities are free. The parks are open year round with a wide range of facilities. What really touched me was that there were so many activities led by volunteers who had a passion, and were eager to share it with others. Every time I went out in search of an activity, I met people who had endless stories about what they loved to do, and how they got interested in a certain hobby, park, or nature spot. The friends groups of the parks sponsor hundreds of events that are open to anyone who shares their passion for the parks. Some of those people are featured in my photos you see in this book. By the way, all the photos are my own. These are real local people.

There are a few tools I used to find the information I write about here. I use an iPhone application called **Oh Ranger! Park Finder**. It allows you to find parks near you from wherever you are currently. It was easy enough to get a list of Milwaukee county parks from their website, but many of the local city and village parks take a little more detective work. You can also select a park by activity. I also subscribe to more than 100 different Facebook pages related to local businesses that support the parks, as well as the parks along with their friends' groups. By doing this, I get real time photos and information about events in my newsfeed every day. **OnMilwaukee** is another useful resource as they offer reviews and list events. **JSOnline** often has park events or compilations of activities at places in parks that I use. I sometimes find useful information in their weekend updates. Of course, the website for Milwaukee County Parks is the best resource for all county park events and activities. I truly appreciate these websites and the people who write for them. I received no compensation from any park or business listed here. These are my own personal observations and opinions.

As you will see, I use the term Milwaukee parks rather loosely. I include a wide variety of outdoor activities that include the waterfront, Lake Michigan, museum roofs, public gardens, and even cemeteries. It's all good fun, even though my definition may not be the same as yours.

I hope this book will get you out into the parks and encourage you to try something new. It's all there just waiting for YOU. The activities are listed in alphabetical order. Everything was current when written, but volunteers run so many programs that there are bound to be changes in the future. Hope you have as much fun trying them as I've had discovering them.

ADAPTIVE SPORTS AND PLAY

The Milwaukee City Recreation Department has a complete program of adaptive sports for people with orthopedic, visual, and other physical or health impairments. Youth and adults are able to enjoy swimming, track & field, power soccer, goal ball, and more. For innovative, enriching, and competitive athletics, call (414)647-6043. www.milwaukeerecreation.net

Three Milwaukee county facilities offer year round social and recreational opportunities, especially designed for residents with physical and developmental disabilities. There is also a Rec Room run by the Office of Disabilities. For their calendar, which includes the Wil-O-Way, events, go to www.county.milwaukee.gov/OPD

Holler Park, 5151 S. 6th St.
Wil-O-Way Underwood, 10602 Underwood Parkway
Wil-O-Way Grant, 207 Lake Dr.

Wil-O-Way Grant Park has a playground that is accessible, right next to the recreation building. You can also find an accessible disc golf course at this park. Washington Park has an accessible playground at the northeast corner.

ARCHERY

You will need to bring your own bows, arrows, and targets, but the hay bales are available at the county ranges at the following parks:
Kinnickinnic River Parkway, S. 20th St, and Kinnickinnic River Parkway
Kletzsch, 6560 N. Milwaukee River Parkway
Root River Parkway (near Whitnall Park), S 92nd St, north of Rawson Ave.
Little Menomonee River Parkway, between Appleton Ave & Mill Rd.
Warnimont, 5400 S. Lake Dr.

These are the only Milwaukee parks where you can use bows and arrows lawfully.

ART

The parks are full of inspiration for artists. We have beautiful bridges, stone arches, waterfalls, sculptures, and lovely scenery in all seasons. If you're an artist, you only have to get out and look. And in fact, you can even get inspiration through the Milwaukee Parks pinterest board, if that's more your style.

Of special interest are the beautiful huge murals that cover the Menomonee Valley passage from the Hank Aaron Trail to the Urban Ecology Center. Painted by artist, Chad Brady, they are colorful and tell the stories of Miller Park area, Potawatomi Casino, the Brewers, The Milwaukee Road, bridges, buildings, animal life, and the people who live in the area. The best way to see it is in person.

The Milwaukee Art Museum holds the Lakefront Art Festival every June. The park-like grounds are turned into an art extravaganza where you can purchase everything from jewelry to hand carved furniture. You'll see a wide variety of local artists at this event, and it offers children an opportunity to make a slew of creative art projects to take home. They have an entire tent dedicated to fostering creativity in children for the duration of the festival. You will also find jugglers, mimes, and face painting. I especially like the garden displays and sand sculptures that are created for this event. We never miss it if we're in town. www.lfoa.mam.org

The Artists Working in Education Van is a mobile art studio that makes the rounds of the parks during the summer. They put out a schedule online in early summer. It's a drop in program for school age kids. They provide the materials, young adults who act as coaches, and loads of creativity for projects that can be completed in a day, usually around a weekly theme. They also do group projects like murals. What kid wouldn't enjoy going to the park to play and finding tables full of fascinating crafts too? During the fall months, you will likely find them at local libraries. www.awe-inc.org

The Milwaukee Domes, at Mitchell Park, hosts an art festival each year in August. It's a fundraiser for the Domes, and is a highlight for art lovers. There are plein air artists as well as exhibiting artists, children's activities, and entertainment. www.milwaukeedomesartfestival.com

ASTRONOMY

If you are interested in studying the heavens, you can join the Wehr Astronomical Society, Inc. at one of their meetings or events. They meet the 2nd Tuesday of every month, usually at the Wehr, Nature Center, 9701 W. College Ave. (414)425-8550. The group uses an observatory at Froemming Park, 8801 S. 51st., Franklin. Park in the parking lot on the west side of 51st Street and then walk west for 400 feet to the observatory. All sessions are free and open to the public. www.wehrastro.org
There's another observatory in New Berlin, the Milwaukee Astronomical Society Observatory. They have a number of high-powered telescopes and their events are open to the public. www.milwaukeeastro.org

If you need a little help identifying stars before you head out on your own to look at the heavens, You might want to consider a stop at the Manfred Olson Planetarium. For just $2 you can see a show on Fridays from 7-8 pm. The programs change every 4-6 weeks. They also have free stargazing with the telescopes on weeknights throughout the year.
1900 E. Kenwood Blvd, Physics Building
www4.uwm.edu/planetarium/shows/

BEACH SWIM

Milwaukee lakeshore beaches are used for swimming during the summer, but not all have lifeguards. The beaches are monitored for water quality during the swimming season. You can check the county beaches website for water quality reports, or look for signs posted at the beaches, if it is unsafe to swim. At this website, you can also check today's weather forecast, UV index, and air quality. www.milwaukeecountybeaches.org

Over the past few years as they noticed ecoli present in the water along the beaches, they looked for a way to improve it. Infiltration basins at the storm sewer outfalls along Bradford Beach were installed. Natural treatments such as sand dunes with native beach plantings at the outfalls, as well as rain gardens up in Lake Park above Bradford Beach were planted. Now we'll see if this improves the water quality for Bradford Beach. South Shore Beach was listed as one of the worst beaches along Lake Michigan for water quality over the past few years, in spite of efforts to reduce bacteria through the use of rain gardens. There has been some discussion about moving the beach away from the marina. Use caution when swimming and avoid the water after a heavy rainstorm when bacteria levels tend to be higher.

There's an app you can download to your phone that makes it easy to find, explore, and enjoy your local beaches. The app **Waterkeeper Swim Guide** was developed by the innovative people at Lake Ontario Waterkeeper and is now managed by Milwaukee Riverkeeper and other member groups of the Waterkeeper Alliance, a network of 200 water protection groups worldwide. You click on the beach you want to know about, and it gives you information about water quality, not only here in Milwaukee but wherever you travel. It also includes a brief description and photos submitted by users.

List of Milwaukee Beaches:
Atwater Park Beach, Capitol at Lake Dr., Shorewood
Bay View Beach, 3120 S. Lake Dr.
Bender Beach, 4503 E. Ryan Rd., Oak Creek
Bradford Beach, 2400 N. Lincoln Memorial Dr.
Grant Park Beach, 100 S. Hawthorne Ave., South Milwaukee
McKinley Beach, 1750 N. Lincoln Memorial Drive
South Shore Beach, 2900 S. Superior St.
Tietjen Beach/Doctor's Park Beach, 1870 E. Fox Lane, Fox Point
Klode Park, 5900 N. Lake Dr., Whitefish Bay
Brown Deer has The Village Pond, 4920 W. Green Brook Dr. that is a one-acre chlorinated swimming facility with a sand beach.

Bradford Beach is considered the best beach for activities in Milwaukee. They have lifeguards. The beach is cleaned regularly. You can play volleyball and have lunch and drinks at the historic beach house. Cabanas are for rent. Parking is usually difficult to find, so you're encouraged to bus, bike, or take the Bradford Beach Shuttle, which runs hourly between Discovery World, Ryan Braun's Graffito, and Bradford Beach. www.bradfordbeachjam.com

The Polar Bear Plunge is unique enough to be included on some people's bucket lists, and requires a bit of thick skin and real planning to do it well. It's not really a swimming event, more than it is an opportunity to thrash in the semi-frozen Lake Michigan with hundreds of people cheering you on. It's held every January 1st at Bradford Beach with the plunge at noon. People who have done this say it's a good idea to bring loose fitting clothes or a robe you can put on after you leave the water. You'll also need towels, blankets, and maybe a few heating packs for your hands and feet. There are some participants who put up tents and have sleeping bags on hand to warm up. The event is free. You don't need to have a reservation, so you can be spontaneous. There are shuttles at many of the area bars. Parking is limited. Spectators are welcome. There is free hot chocolate until it runs out. www.polarplungemilwaukee.com

BEACH & SAND VOLLEYBALL

For many years our beaches were neglected, but life came back to them and Bradford Beach has become the pinnacle of summer entertainment. As you pass by in summer, you'll see rows of volleyball nets. There are national tournaments for beach volleyball held here, as well as games for fun. You can rent their equipment or join a league. They even have youth events. www.bradfordbeachjam.com

There are additional sand volleyball areas at:
Konkel Park, 5151 W. Layton Ave., Greenfield.
Brown Deer Park, 7835 N. Green Bay Rd.
Dretzka, 12020 W. Bradley Rd.
Estabrook, 4400 N. Estabrook Dr.
Froemming, 8801 S. 51st St.
Greenfield, 2028 S. 124th St.
Kletzsch, 6560 N. Milwaukee River Parkway
Lincoln, 1301 W. Hampton Ave.
Madison, 9800 W. Glendale Ave.
McCarty, 8214 W. Cleveland Ave.
McGovern, 5400 N. 51st St.
Mitchell, S 22nd St & W. Pierce St.
Root River Parkway, Picnic Areas #1 & #3
Sheridan, 4800 S. Lake Dr.
South Shore, 2900 S. Shore Dr.
Wilson Recreation Center, 4001 S. 20th St.

BEER GARDEN

Beer gardens are a relatively new addition to the parks, but have been received with enthusiasm. Estabrook's 'Biergarten" was named a top 10 beer garden in the WORLD, by Cheap Flights. How lucky are we to have it in our own back yard?! The way a beer garden works, is that you can bring your own mug if you like. They fill it up for you. Tables are shared with other patrons. There is food for sale, or you can bring your own picnic. If you prefer, you can "rent" a mug for a nominal fee, which is returned when you return the mug. There is live music sometimes, and also a great view of the Milwaukee River from the patio. The Estabrook Beer Garden is located at 4600 Estabrook Drive.

www.oldgermanbeerhall.com/estabrook-beer-garden

Hoyt Park also has a beer garden, with similar rules and food, at The Landing, run by the Friends of Hoyt Park. Proceeds from the sale of food and beverages here go directly to supporting the pool and park. 1800 N. Swan Blvd, Wauwatosa. (414)302-9160. www.friendsofhoytpark.org.

BIKE

Wisconsin is known for bicycling, and Milwaukee is especially bike friendly with its network of more than 55 miles of bike lanes, 50 miles of bike paths, and 100 miles of designated on street bike routes. The Oak Leaf trail and the Hank Aaron Trail are the two largest, longest trail systems that accommodate bicycles. The Oak Leaf trail runs north to south, through all of the lakefront parks, and some of the river front parks. It was voted the best urban bike trail in 2012. The Hank Aaron Trail runs east to west, and brings you from the lakefront out towards Brewers stadium. For the best and most current information about conditions, pick up a "Milwaukee by Bike" map at one of the local bicycle shops. The Bicycle Federation of Wisconsin produces it. The Wisconsin Bike Federation and the Milwaukee Bicycle Community are also responsible for organizing fun rides, such as the Santa Rampage and the Tour de Fat. They are a great resource for information on all topics bike related. Browse their websites to see what services they provide. www.wisconsinbikefed.org. www.mkebke.com

Travel Wisconsin has many great guides you can download or request online. One of them is the Wisconsin Biking Guide. It includes a few spots near Milwaukee, but also has information about biking all over Wisconsin. http://www.travelwisconsin.com/order-guides

If you plan to bike the Oak Leaf Trail, you may want to get a passport for the Oak Leaf Discovery Tour, a fun program run by the Park People, which encourages you to visit parks along the trail. You can collect stamps and secret words from 24 parks along the 115-mile trail, and then at the end of the summer, you submit your completed passport (with 8 stamps or a combination of stamps and secret words) for a chance in prizes at their end of season party. www.parkpeoplemke.org

Do you enjoy biking with a social group? If so, you might like to check out the Sitzmarks of Milwaukee. They have weekly rides of 15-18 miles on Wednesdays from Greenfield Park during summer. You have to join the club and must be 21. www.sitzmark.org Local bike shops also know about other groups that ride on a regular basis.

If you're visiting the area and want an organized bicycle tour of the city, contact Whirlwind Bike Trips and Rentals, 2410 N. Murray Ave. (414)967-9446 or Brew City Bike Tours, 2108 N. Farwell Ave., (414)336-9610.

You can rent hybrid mountain bicycles and tandems at the lakefront Veteran's Park, from Milwaukee Bike & Skate. They are open seasonally, Memorial Day-Labor Day.
They have surrey bikes that hold 2-8 people in 2 different sizes. There are turbos, which are recumbent trikes. These bikes require you to use your shifting body weight and feet to steer. Handlebars are for holding on as you cruise the lakefront. They also have skelters, which are a form of go-kart. Rental is by the half hour. 1500 N. Lincoln Memorial Dr. (414)273-1343 www.milwbikeskaterental.com

Milwaukee is in its infancy with a bike share program that was launched with a kiosk at Discovery World in 2013. With this system, you can rent a bike hourly using a credit card, and eventually you will be able to bike around town and return bikes at kiosks in other locations. A non-profit corporation, Midwest Bikeshare,Inc, runs the program. The goal is to install 25 kiosks and 250 BikeShare bicycles in the metro Milwaukee area by Spring 2014.

The Urban Ecology Center runs a series of bicycle courses and organized rides, starting from their neighborhood centers located at parks. For information about current events, visit their website www.urbanecologycenter.org.

Bayshore Town Center sometimes organizes area bike rides. For current information, check their website under events.. www.bayshoretowncenter.com

Havenwoods State Forest has about 2 miles of limestone trails and asphalt roads that are open to bicycles. These are shared trails, so watch for hikers.

There are mixed opinions about mountain biking on shared trails in Milwaukee. Bikes are not allowed on the unpaved river trails due to concerns over erosion. There is an avid group of Milwaukee mountain bikers, Metro Mountain Bikers, who work to ensure trails are available, and they can be a resource for current works in progress. They also organize regular rides if you enjoy riding in a group setting.
www.metromountainbikers.com

Here are a couple of mountain biking routes:
Alpha Mountain Bike Trail. Trailhead 6740 S. 92nd St. Located at the toboggan hill in Whitnall Park's winter sports area (northeast of the golf course). If you are driving to the trail, park at the Whitnall golf course lot, 6751 S. 92nd St, and ride your bike northeast to the trailhead. This is a 3 mile single-track narrow trail that heads eastward to the to the Root River Parkway. The trail has only a few steep or rocky segments.

Hoyt Mountain Bike Trail. Trailhead 1800 Swan Blvd, near the entrance parking lot. This trail is a 2.5-mile loop. There are points to this trail that provide a definite challenge. Winding along the Menomonee River, this scenic trail is primarily single track, with one way for bike and the other for pedestrians.

If you're looking for something a bit more adventurous, the Rock Sports Complex, near Whitnall Park, is a new facility with 7 miles of cross country and single-track mountain bike trails. Trail passes are needed for trail use, but they do have networks to free trails throughout Whitnall Park. 7900 W. Crystal Ridge Dr., Franklin.. You can see trail maps and get more information about fees and rentals at www.rockcomplex.com/bike-parks/

BIKE-IN MOVIE NIGHTS

You've heard of drive-in movies? We have bike-in movies outdoors at the Swing Park underneath the Holton Street Bridge. There are normally 3-5 movies per season, and you can find the line-up at www.mkebke.com. The movies are free. If you are unfamiliar with this park, it's easiest to look for Trocadero Gastrobar at 1758. N. Water St. or from the other side of the river, you can access it from the pedestrian bridge right by Lakefront Brewery, 1872. N. Commerce..

BIKE PARK

The Rock Sports Complex is the place to try out a variety of unique biking. Their overall theme is to be "bigger, badder, and better" than any other facilities in the nation, and offer a variety of extreme sports as well as team sports. For those who love trying new sports, this is worth a visit.

New to The Rock is a pro spec BMX racetrack, which is the 2nd largest BMX track in the United States. The track features doubles, step-ups, and rollers for fast qualifying times. This track will gear towards all ages and abilities. They welcome all types of riders, novice to professional. Starting in spring, they will offer clinics by professionals for riders of all levels, to increase technique and performance.

They also offer Gravity Biking, which is one of four Gravity Bike courses in the United States, and one of seven in North America. You can rent full suspension mountain bikes with hydraulic brakes, or you can bring your own. The course is seasonal, as later in the year, the hill is used for snow sports. You will find runs ranked by difficulty (green, blue, black, and double black). You will also find a variety of trails designed for mountain biking. The hill has plenty of downhill runs, flow trails, and pump tracks for all bike enthusiasts. We can't compete vertically with the hills out west, but we can compete with top tier all terrain parks. 7900 Crystal Ridge, Franklin (414)529-7676

BIKE POLO

Bike polo is more like hockey on bikes, than traditional polo. It's played on hard courts with 2 teams and a goal at each end. The object of the game is to score goals by hitting the ball into the net. The Milwaukee Bike Polo Club plays at Washington Park, 4100 W. Vliet St. It's a recurring event on Sundays throughout summer and fall at 1 pm until dark. While you could potentially use any bike, most of the bicycles being used are built here in Milwaukee specifically for the sport by Ben's Cycle, 1018 W. Lincoln Ave. The spokes are often covered to prevent a mallet from going through the wheel. Stop by to watch a practice session and see if it's for you. For more information, contact the Milwaukee Bike Polo Club at www.milwaukeebikepolo.com.

BIRDS

You don't have to be an expert to enjoy looking for birds. Seven Milwaukee county communities are already considered official "Bird Cities" – Fox Point, Bayside, River Hills, Hales Corners, Milwaukee, Shorewood, and Whitefish Bay. This part of the state is on a migration path. The best way to spot birds? Get a good pair of binoculars, and head out to one of the parks. You can see birds everywhere. Look up. Look down. Look on the water.

You can join a warbler walk at Lake Park, where the feeders are well stocked, and the habitat supreme for bird life. If you're very lucky, you may spot the family of turkeys that live in Lake Park. Or come in early morning and watch the peregrine falcons catching prey. There's a Duck Watch monthly during fall and early winter. You can find times on the Lake Park Friends website. Usually they meet on a Saturday at North Point, just north of Bradford Beach, from 11-1. With this group, you'll learn more about sea birds (and others) from a local expert. These are informal and open to all ages and levels of birding experience. 3233 E. Kenwood Blvd. www.lakeparkfriends.org

The Urban Ecology Centers have early morning bird walks a few days per week. Check their events calendar to find one that works for you. www.urbanecologycenter.org

Havenwoods State Forest also has a birding group that meets weekly for walks. The nature center staff will even lend you binoculars and a bird identification book while you hike their trails.
http://dnr.wi.gov/topic/parks/name/havenwoods/

If it's raptors you crave, the Schlitz Audubon Nature Center has one of the best raptor programs in the area. They have 16 raptors living in the center, including eagles, owls, and falcons. which are cared for by staff and volunteers. They make scheduled appearances both at the center and at community events. Check the calendar to see where you may find them. 1111 E. Brown Deer Rd. www.sanc.org

You can also participate in a bird count. They are often held in December at parks, and in February from your own backyard. Usually the Schlitz Audubon Center, Lake Park Friends, Urban Ecology Center, or Wehr Nature Centers host events for this project.

The Great Wisconsin Birding & Nature Trail maps out the best locations in Wisconsin to see birds. It's meant to be driven by automobile, but naturally you have to get out of the car at the destinations listed to take a good look at what is there. Several Milwaukee parks are listed. You can see a PDF version at http://www.travelwisconsin.com/pdf/lake_michigan_guide.pdf Or get more information about the trails at www.wisconsinbirds.org

A checklist of Wisconsin birds is available from the DNR. Print this out and put it in your pocket to keep track of what you see. www.dnr.state.wi.us

BOAT RIDES

If you like being on the water, a boat ride on the river or lakefront is one of the best ways to see Milwaukee during the summer. Most run May-September. When you're stumped for a great gift idea, the boat lines also offer gift certificates.

There are guided boat tours nearly every day of the week, and the emphasis of the tour changes, so be sure to find something that suits the needs of your group. There are 3 boat vendors in Milwaukee, and I've listed them below. Watch groupon for local deals on boat tours too.

Riverwalk Boat Tours & Rentals is at Pere Marquette Park. They do pub-crawls, brewery tours, and even fireworks tours while the festivals are on. You can also rent a 21-foot pontoon boat, but you must complete a boater safety course and be over 18. www.riverwalkboats.com

Milwaukee Boat Line does the river, harbor, and lake Michigan. You can take the narrated history & trivia cruises to explore Milwaukee's past & present. There are concert cruises, and cruises that include dinner or brunch. They can be found on the river walk at 101 W. Michigan St. www.mkeboat.com

The Milwaukee River Cruise Line has historic tours, cruises with food, and most importantly to families- they have kid friendly cruises. Be sure to check out the information on the Caribbean Pirate cruise if you have kids that enjoy wearing pirate costumes. The 90-minute tour includes food that kids would eat, as well as an opportunity to defend the vessel from pirates. These tours depart from 205 W. Highland Avenue. They also have one of the newest, largest, double-decker sightseeing boats. You can rent your own pontoon boat here as well. Rates vary by number of hours and day of week. It can hold up to 10 passengers and you are the pilot. You must be 23 and have a valid driver's license. www.edelweissboats.com

For something really different, sail on the **Denis Sullivan**, which sets off from Discovery World. This ship is a recreation of a 19th century three masted Great Lakes schooner that was built in 2000 by professional shipwrights and nearly 1000 volunteers. There are a variety of tours, from a 2-hour lake watch to multi-day educational sails for teens and adults. 500 N. Harbor Dr. (414)765-8640 www.discoveryworld.org

BONFIRES

Bonfires aren't allowed by private citizens on Milwaukee's beaches, however there are two places you're likely to find summer beach bonfires. Lakeshore State Park often holds family friendly educational programs, hosted by rangers that include a bonfire near the lagoon. They normally advertise this on their Facebook page. The other place for bonfires is Bradford Beach, when they host bonfires with music, which tend to be more adult oriented. www.bradfordbeachjam.com

The Urban Ecology Centers have fires at their outdoor pits. Check the website for events to find one near you. www.urbanecologycenter.org

If you want to make your own bonfires, there's a pit at Hawthorn Glen at picnic area 1. Call to make reservations, (414)647-6050. You'll need to bring your own firewood. 1130 N. 60th St.

Havenwoods State Forests has bonfires in conjunction with special weekend activities. 6141 N. Hopkins St. (414)527-0232.

BOOKS & STORY HOURS

Of course, you can always bring your own books and settle on a bench under a shade tree. Lake Park Friends have organized the installation of attractive memorial benches along pathways throughout the park. They are called Olmsted Poet's Walk park benches, after the famous architect of parks, Frederick Law Olmsted. He designed many parks in the United States, including Lake Park and Central Park., NYC. The benches in Lake Park are the same ones they have in Central Park, and each has a poem inscription. It's fun to walk through the park reading the interesting poems. One of my favorites, "Just living is not enough…One must have sunshine, freedom, and a little flower.-Hans Christian Andersen."

During summer, story times are held at Lake Park (hosted by COA), Lakeshore State Park, and at the Wehr Nature Center. Times and dates are generally available on the individual park websites. Wehr Nature Center also has a year round program for 2-3 year olds, called Little Wonders, which includes story time, a craft, a walk, and a snack.

Havenwoods State Forest has a preschool story time every other Tuesday. These programs are for ages 3-5 and their accompanying adults. They are not for day care centers. They have a Junior Ranger Program during summer, which includes a story, hike and project for ages 6-8. 6141 N. Hopkins St. www.friendsofhavenwoods.org

If you'd like to pick up a few books and do reading in a park on your own, there are free libraries popping up in the parks and surrounding neighborhoods. It seems impossible to keep up with all of them, but I know they are located at these parks:
Kletzsch Park playground, 6560 N. Milwaukee River Pkwy.
South Shore Park playground, 2900 South Shore Dr.
Ellsworth Park playground, 600 Ellsworth Ln., Bayside
LaFollette Park, 9418 W. Washington St., West Allis
Wehr Nature Center, 9701 W. College Ave., Franklin
Jewell Park, S. 19th St & W. Wood Ave.

BRUNCH

Bartolotta runs the restaurant at **Lake Park Bistro,** at Lake Park. 3133 E. Newberry Blvd. They do a Sunday brunch from 10-2, which is a 3-course meal. You choose your courses off the menu and pay accordingly. You can get champagne, mimosas, bloody Mary drinks, as well as juices. The eggs benedict and croque madame come highly recommended! They even have a children's menu, which is also 3 courses. You can make a reservation, but it is not required. (414)962-6300

Boerner Botanical Gardens has had weekend brunch in the past, but they are advertising a new caterer in 2014, so stay tuned.

Hubbard Park Lodge in Shorewood is another favorite brunch place. It's a rustic lodge in a beautiful park setting along the Milwaukee River. The brunch is a "lumberjack menu" which is hearty and served family style. The fried doughnuts they bring you when you arrive are fabulous. And then it continues to get better as you taste pancakes, eggs, hash browns, and breakfast sausages or bacon. It is served every Sunday from 9-2. This is a great place for the whole family and it's affordable. You don't need a reservation for this casual brunch. Just drop in! 3565 N. Morris. (414)332-4207

CEMETERY TOURS

Heading out to a cemetery may seem queer, but we have some quite famous Milwaukeeans buried in a few of our famous cemeteries, and the tombs are quite impressive in a park like setting. My own son was disappointed that there were no zombies, but once you get past that, it can be very interesting.

If you know the history of cemeteries in general, it will help you understand why I've included them here in a book about parks. They were first started by creating large parcels of land, typically outside the city limits and owned by the city or town. They were frequently used as parks, where family members would visit and picnic while tending to the family graves. As much care went into landscaping them as did parks of that era. In fact, few people may be aware that Frederick Law Olmsted also designed cemeteries.

Forest Home Cemetery is the place where many of Milwaukee's famous fathers are buried along with their families. The cemetery was founded in 1850 on land that used to be a farm. It is now 200 acres of rolling land with flowering trees, shrubs, and greenery. With 150 years of burials, the stones themselves are quite interesting to see. The most significant people don't necessarily have the grandest burial plots.

You can do a self-guided historical tour at any time by downloading the map and the information about the people buried there. Because it's such a large cemetery, you can drive around the cemetery, park your car, and walk to the well-marked lots and find the specific stones. Or each month, volunteers take visitors on tours of the cemetery, pointing out various graves and telling the stories behind the people who are buried there. They typically have tours for early mayors, beer barons, and civil war heroes. The Halls of history should be the starting place for any tour. It's a building near the entrance and is well marked with that name on the side of the building. Go downstairs where you can see the photos and stories of many famous Milwaukeeans who are buried there. You can also find restrooms and drinking fountain there. If you walk across the street from this building, you will see stairs down to a garden, and at the top of the other side is a pretty chapel. The landscaping throughout the cemetery is well done and maintained. You can drive over beautiful stone bridges, see a pond and waterfall, and enjoy the plants and memorials. (414)645-2632 www.foresthomecemetery.com/historical.html

Calvary Cemetery is a catholic cemetery, dating from 1856. It has some famous Milwaukeeans, civil war veterans, beer barons, and interesting structures. 5503 W. Bluemound Rd. Download a self guided tour at www.cemeteries.org

Wood National Cemetery, 5000 W. National Ave, is located on the grounds of a former Soldiers Home that today is called the Clement J. Zablocki VA Medical Center.
From 1867 until 1871, the home buried its soldiers in private cemeteries in the Milwaukee area. In 1871, a cemetery opened on the grounds. Originally known only as Soldiers Home Cemetery, it wasn't until 1937 the name was changed to honor Gen. George Wood, a longtime member of the Soldiers' Home's Board of Managers. It became a national cemetery in 1973.
The cemetery is part of the Northwestern Branch-National Home for Disabled Volunteer Soldiers National Historic Landmark district,

designated on June 6, 2011.The 60-foot-tall granite Civil War Soldiers and Sailors monument was erected in 1903 when the cemetery was part of the Northwest Branch Asylum for Disabled Volunteer Soldiers. The monument was sponsored by the Soldiers and Sailors Association and was sculpted by Joseph Shaver Granite and Marble Co. of Milwaukee.
A memorial pathway is lined with a variety of memorials that honor America's veterans. As of 2003, there were seven memorials along there — most commemorating soldiers of 20th-century wars.

CHESS

There is a permanent, outdoor chess table, created by Kevin Oulahan, in the pocket park at 3rd St. & Walker in Walker's Point. You'd have to bring your own chairs and chess pieces, but the board is just waiting for players. Also in the park are several benches, picnic tables, and a HUGE rock, called Stone Bracelet by Zoran Mojsilov. This could be an ideal quiet place for you to play.

CIVIL WAR REENACTMENTS

There are generally two places that host war reenactments in Milwaukee, however you may see groups of reenactors participating in holiday parades. Reclaiming our Heritage has traditionally used the Zablocki VA Medical Center grounds, however they took a year off due to construction at the grounds. To follow their event updates go to www.forohmilwaukee.org

Trimborn Farm is another location used for civil war reenactments. 8881 W. Grange Ave, Greendale. This park is only open sunrise to sunset, May 15-Oct 15. To find out dates for the current year, call the Milwaukee County Historical Society. (414)273-8288.

CLEANUPS & WEED-OUTS

If you want to help maintain the parks' natural areas, there are a number of cleanups throughout the year. We have a serious problem with garlic mustard, buckthorn, and other invasive species. Many parks set up their own weed-out campaign, but the most comprehensive information may be available through the Park People. While we're getting rid of unwanted plants in the parks, it's a good time to consider what replaces them. If you would like to plant a tree, the Park People can obtain ornamentals, evergreens, and shade trees. You can donate to purchase a tree and know that future generations will enjoy it. www.parkpeoplemke.org

The Milwaukee River keeper group organizes events for the river, including an annual river cleanup in spring. They recruit volunteers who pull out thousands of pounds of garbage for the waterways and surrounding banks, improving habitat for wildlife. 1845 N. Farwell Ave., Suite 100 (414)287-0207 www.mkeriverkeeper.org

CURLING

Wisconsin has a long tradition of curling. There are more clubs in Wisconsin than in any other state in the nation. The Wauwatosa Curling Club is a place for men and women of all ages. The Curling Club is located in Hart Park in the Muellner Building, where members play on four sheets of ice. All games are followed by the tradition of broom stacking, where members of both teams hang out and socialize. Members of the club are responsible for paying annual dues. Every member gets a locker, and first- and second-year curlers receive discounts. Guests are welcome and basic curling instruction is available. www.wauwatosacurlingclub.com

The Milwaukee Curling Club, has a new facility in Ozaukee County at the fairgrounds, W67N890 Washington Ave, Cedarburg. www.milwaukeecurlingclub.com

CROSS COUNTRY SKI

If snow is 6" deep, the county cross country trails will be groomed at Brown Deer Park, 7835 N. Green Bay Rd. (414)352-7502, and Whitnall Park, 6751 S. 92nd St. (414)425-1810.

Brown Deer Park has 4.5 miles of trails groomed for skate/freestyle, and classical/diagonal skiers of all levels. It's a flat gentle terrain with open areas and woods. There are toilets open during the day near the skating rink. The park is open sunrise to 10 pm. Call the office for ski rental.

Whitnall Park has 5.6 miles of trails groomed for classical/diagonal skiers of all levels. There is gentle, rolling terrain with woods and open fields. You will find concessions and a warming house (golf clubhouse) with restrooms. Call the clubhouse for ski rentals.

Schlitz Audubon Center has groomed trails. This is a fee area. 1111 E. Brown Deer Rd. www.sanc.org

The urban ecology centers also have cross country skis, boots, and poles for rent. They come in a variety of sizes for kids and adults. www.urbanecologycenter.org

Havenwoods State Forest offers 2 miles of flat trails for shared Cross Country skiing and snowshoeing. 6141 N Hopkins St. (414)527-0232 The Kettle Moraine Forest isn't that far away either. www.dnr.wi.gov

CUSTARD & BURGERS

North Point Custard is on the lakefront next to Bradford Beach, advertising delicious frozen custard, burgers, fries, and shakes. This snack stand is part of the Bartolotta restaurant group, which is a Milwaukee icon. Expect grilled burgers on toasted buns, with a variety of toppings stuffed in between. There are other options as well. You can have a bratwurst or chicken sandwich. Everything is cooked to order, so expect to wait in line. The crinkle fries are a big hit, but you can also opt for onion rings. Don't miss out on dessert. The custard (which is different than ice cream) is creamy and tasty. The sizes are a bit on the large side, so order accordingly. Seems a shame to waste even a bite. Only open May-October. 2272 N. Lincoln Memorial Dr., (414)727-4886

CYCLOCROSS

Cyclocross is gaining in popularity here in Wisconsin. It's a form of bike racing with some adventure added. You find yourself riding in the grass, dismounting to get around obstacles, riding like the wind through fields and hills! It's typically a fall season sport and the racecourses are often set up in the parks here in Milwaukee, using tape and poles. Each race is 30-90 minutes. It tests aerobic endurance and bike handling skills. Races have been held in Mitchell Park, Estabrook Park, and Doyne Park, but they could be held anywhere. To follow the sport, or to join in the fun, contact the Wisconsin Cycling Association. They can tell you where to find clinics and support. www.wicycling.org

DISC GOLF

There are currently 8 disc golf courses in the Milwaukee county parks, and the Great Lakes Disc Golf Association runs most. You have to bring your own discs to play. Here are the courses with the number of holes in parentheses:

Brown Deer, 7625 N. Range Line Rd. (18)

Dineen, 6600 W. Keefe Ave. (18)

Dretzka Park, 12020 W. Bradley Rd. (27)

Estabrook Park, 4400 N. Estabrook Dr. (18)

Kops Park, 3321 N. 86th St. (2)

Milwaukee County Sports Complex, 6000 Ryan Rd. (9)

The Office runs the following 2 courses for Persons with Disabilities (414)278-3938 and use is encouraged by beginners. They are not totally handicapped accessible.

Wil-O-Way Grant, 207 Lake Dr. (3)

Wil-O-Way Underwood, 10602 Underwood Creek Parkway (3)

Oak Creek has an 18 hole disc golf course at Abendschein Park, 1311 E. Drexel Ave., Oak Creek.

DIVE FOR SHIPWRECKS

Over 4700 ships sunk on the Great Lakes, and about 10 are just off the Milwaukee Lake Michigan coastline. Lacking saltwater and corrosive marine organisms found in oceans, the shipwrecks are better preserved in the cold fresh water. You can read about some of the shipwrecks on signs posted at parks along the lakefront, such as Atwater Park in Shorewood. You can also see a map of the shipwrecks along with some additional information about the type of ships that were lost. www.shipwreckexplorers.com/lake_michigan_milwaukee.php

The diving season runs from May to early November, though it is possible to dive in Lake Michigan year round. Lake temperatures during summer are 60-70F. Visibility varies from day to day. Sometimes you can see 100 feet, but generally it's more like 35 feet. Storms greatly affect visibility.

Aquatic Adventures, Inc. can take you shipwreck diving to see the local wrecks. They also offer a variety of scuba lessons. (262)938-6827 www.dive-aai.com

Adventure Charter boats LLC and the local dive shops have teamed up to offer a shipwreck diving experience. McKinley Marina (414)339-5090

If you enjoy learning about the ships that were lost on Lake Michigan, you might also want to drive the Schooner Coast tour which runs from Manitowoc to Door County and includes the maritime museums, historic village at Two Rivers, lighthouses, and several maritime vessels. www.schoonercoast.org

DOGS

Dogs aren't allowed on any of the lakefront beaches and there is a fine of about $200 if you are caught with a dog on the beach.

There are fenced in dog exercise areas, run by the county, but you need a permit, and a dog license to use them. You'll need proof of rabies vaccination to get the permit. They are open 7 days a week, 5am-10pm

Currie, 3535 N. Mayfair Rd.

Granville, 11718 W. Good Hope Place

Estabrook, 4400 N. Estabrook Dr.

Runway, 1214 E. Rawson Ave.

Warnimont, 6100 S. Lake Dr.

Any Pit Bull in the dog exercise area at Warnimont must have a bright orange collar and must be leashed with a leash 4' or shorter, and be accompanied by a person 16 years or older. For more information from users of the parks, go to www.milwaukeedogparks.org

There are at least 2 more that are under construction currently. Bay View will have a park at the corner of Lincoln Ave and Bay St. Riverwest's new dog park (called Roverwest) will be in the block between Concordia, Auer, Bremen, and Weil.

The Oak Leaf Trail is dog friendly, but dogs must be on a leash because it is a shared use trail.

Havenwoods State Forest welcomes dogs in the forested areas as long as they remain on a leash 8 feet or shorter. There is a specially marked Pet Trail that is 2 ½ miles long.

If you don't mind heading a bit north of the county line, there's a free run dog park called Katherine Kearney Carpenter Dog Park, 801 W. Zedler, in Mequon. This is a partially wooded area that includes a stream. There are 2 parking lots and a large field for throwing balls.

There are at least 3 really fun events in parks for dog lovers. Watch for notice in the fall for the doggie dip day at a couple of the county park pools before they empty them for the season. There is also a Barktoberfest at Estabrook Park, near the Biergarten. Pugfest is one of the cutest and most fun experiences ever, even if you don't have a pug. They have costume contests, lots of vendors, and freebies for pet owners. This fundraiser for pug rescue is held at the County Sports Complex annually.
www.milwaukeepugfest.com

DOGSLED

Under certain weather conditions, there will be dog sledding available at Whitnall Park on weekends, 11am-1pm, January through March, and possibly Veteran's Park too. The dogs are part of a non-profit recreational dog sled team, Door County Sled Dogs. All of these lovely animals are rescued dogs. To find out when and where they will be, call the hotline during winter months at (414)967-9677. Generally they need 6" of fresh snow. For your donation of $15, you get to visit with the dogs, talk to mushers, and have a short ride in the park. It makes for a great photo. Meet at the golf course warming house, 5879 S. 92nd St., Franklin. www.doorcountysleddogs.com

ETHNIC (AND OTHER) FESTIVALS

The Maier Festival Park is the official location for most ethnic festivals during summer. This park also hosts Pridefest and Summerfest. There are even apps for Summerfest and Festa Italiana at ITunes. Festa Italiana, the very first ethnic festival ever held on the Summerfest grounds, was recently listed by USA Today as a top 10 place to discover Italian Heritage. 200 N. Harbor Dr. www.summerfest.com

There are additional festivals held at other parks.
Bastille Days is held in July at Cathedral Square www.easttown.com
India Fest has been held at Humboldt Park. www.indiafestmilwaukee.org
Global Union hosted by Alverno College is held at Humboldt Park too.
www.alvernopresents.alverno.edu
Milwaukee Highland Games, which celebrates Scots, is at Hart Park, 7300 Chestnut St., Wauwatosa. www.milwaukeescottishfest.com
An annual Lebowski Festival is held at Cathedral Square. It has a cult following and includes a showing of *The Big Lebowski.*
www.lebowskifest.com
Bayview residents are passionate about their South Shore Frolic, held at South Shore Park in July.

EVENT SPACES

If you're planning an event and need a nice place to hold it, there are several historic buildings in the parks that might just be right for you. A park facility like a golf clubhouse could be perfect for the extended family Thanksgiving dinner. How about a garden wedding? Do you need a band shell or auditorium to put on a play or feature your own music? Pool party with the kids more your style? Or perhaps you need to plan an overnight event with a youth group? You can even rent an entire sports complex. For all your needs, there's something for you. There's an incredibly long list with details about fees and hours under rentals. Prices tend to be cheaper than you might pay for privately owned facilities.
www.county.milwaukee.gov

EXERCISE

Boot Camps are held at Bradford Beach, and Klode Park in Whitefish Bay by Milwaukee Adventure Boot Camp from spring to late Fall. There is a fee for this and they run 3-4 weeks of intense fitness instruction, nutritional counseling and motivational training. www.milwaukeebootcamp.com

If you are self-motivated, the parks can be your gym. You can work out all of your major muscle groups using the Helios multigyms that are currently in 13 parks. Your body weight adds resistance to your exercises. The gyms have the following features:

45° back-extension bench

Abdominal-crunch/sit-up bench

Chin-up bar (with chin assist function)
Calf-raise platform
Triceps-dip station (with dip-assist function)

Elevated push-up platform

Cardio thigh-squat station

You can find the multigyms at these parks:
Cannon Park, 303 N 95 St., east of the wading pool
Doctors Park, 1870 E Fox Ln., at the playground
Humboldt Park, 3000 S Howell Ave., between the baseball diamond and the pavilion
Jackson Park, 3500 W Forest Home Ave.
Johnsons Park, 1919 W Fond du Lac Ave., off of 19 St & Brown St.

King Park, 1531 W Vliet St, southeast of the community center
The Lakefront/McKinley Park, 2300 N Lincoln Memorial Dr., near the
Northpoint Snack Bar (This has a total of 20 exercise stations)
Lincoln Park, 1301 W Hampton Ave.
McCarty Park, 8214 W Cleveland Ave., southeast of the wading pool
Mitchell Park, 524 S Layton Blvd., northwest of the wading pool
Scout Lake Park, 5902 W Loomis Rd.
South Shore Park, 2900 S Shore Dr., northeast of the tot lot
Washington Park, 1859 N 40 St., west of the Senior Center

Kosciuszko Community Center has a weight room that is open year round .
You will find free weights, weight machines, exercise bikes, and treadmills.
For women, there's a separate workout area that includes free weights,
exercise bikes, treadmills, and steps. Classes are available in boxing and
martial arts. To use the facility, you need a membership card, which is
bargain priced at $70 per year for a family of 4.   2201 S. 7th St. (414)645-
4624

The Milwaukee County Parks have several senior centers that offer people
aged 50+ an opportunity to socialize and exercise together. There are
fitness centers, which include user-friendly muscle strengthening
equipment, as well as cardiovascular bikes, treadmills, and seated steppers.
Staff from UWM is available at Washington Park Senior Center on a part
time basis to help you get started and provide ongoing assistance. You can
also try Yoga, Tai Chi, or join a walking group. These centers are run by
Interfaith and are sponsored by the Department on Aging. There are no
membership fees, although the activities may require a program fee. For
more information visit their website. http://home.interfaithmilw.org/fun

FALL COLOR

For the finest panoramic view of the area during fall, my park of choice is The Rock Sports Complex. Climb to the top of the ski hill and you will be amazed with the color and beauty .

Many of our parks are planted in hardwood trees that look stunning in fall, depending on weather and moisture conditions. There's a county park fall color tour, that takes a loop through all the lakefront parks, down westwards to Whitnall Park, and up again through all the westerly parks in the county. Although you could technically just drive through the route, you'd miss out on so much by not getting out and doing some walking. These parks have plenty of trails and water features that make them especially scenic. You can pick up an area park map at any county park golf course, or download a pdf file at http://county.milwaukee.gov/ImageLibrary/Groups/cntyParks/trails/map 08fallcolor.pdf

Lynden Sculpture Garden is another very pretty spot in fall. The red trees reflect on the lake and there are nearly always a gaggle of geese just waiting to take flight.

For a day trip, head to Holy Hill in Hubertus, where you can see all the way to Milwaukee. If you go, be sure to take the stairs to the tower for the best views. Another great idea is the Kettle Moraine Scenic driving tour.

FARMERS MARKETS

Farmers Markets in the Milwaukee parks offer you produce fresh from a Wisconsin farm. Vendors offer seasonal produce, plants, cut flowers, and baked goods June through October. All tend to have live music, crafts, and produce. There are many more than those listed here, but these are the ones that are in parks or gardens.

South Shore Park, 2900 South Shore Drive Saturdays 8-12. This has become my favorite "Saturday Park" during the farmer's market season. They have everything you could want. Great top of the bluff location with free on-street parking. Don't bother eating before you come, because you have to try a crepe. The line will be long but oh so worth it. And be sure to say, "Yes please" to the powdered sugar. You can find coffee, snacks, and great fresh produce. The kids can play at the playground. You can pick up a book at the little free library. You'll find plenty of friendly dogs because the Oak Leaf Trail runs through the park. Better yet, you can bike! Plan to stay for a while so you can enjoy the music. www.southshorefarmersmarket.com

Zeidler Union Square, 301 W. Michigan St. Wednesdays, 10-3. This is a charming downtown park with a gazebo and 60 vendors that cater to the downtown lunch crowd.

www.westown.org/neighborhood-events/westown-farmers-market/

Cathedral Square, 520 E. Wells St. Saturdays, 9-1 You can come early and do yoga. Then you'll see a wide variety of fresh produce, baked goods, jewelry, and food trucks. This market is on the small side, but has the essentials. Convenient to ATMs.
www.easttown.com/events/east-town-market

Washington Park, 4420 W. Vliet St. Sundays, 10-2 Held in front of the Senior Center at the park, expect produce, fresh food, artisan crafts, demonstrations, local entertainment. This is the one for kids, as they usually have craft activities. www.westvliet.com/green-market-2 You can also find them on Facebook.

Walker Square, 1031 S. 9th St. Sundays, Tuesdays, and Thursdays 8-5. This one is said to carry the most unusual array of interesting produce, due to the 20 or so Hmong Farmers who sell here. You may find green finger chilies, Asian eggplant, odd greens that don't even translate into American terms, but are tasty, and even corn with fungus. Feel free to ask for cooking suggestions, and they will tell you. You can find them on Facebook.

Riverwest Garden Park, 821 E. Locust St. Sundays, 10-4. It's great to find a market on a Sunday and this is a place for the most excellent people watching. You can pet dogs, admire tattoos, learn about artisan soaps and honey, order organic eggs & meats. They also have the usual fare of produce, herbs, baked goods, music and ridiculously beautiful flowers. www.riverwestmarket.wordpress.com

The award for the highest farmer's market (which is also the newest) goes to Walkers Point, where it is held on the rooftop of the **Clock Shadow Building** among the gardens on Saturdays. 130 W. Bruce St.

Even when winter comes, there is a place you can go for fresh produce, bakery, elk steaks and dairy products. Every Saturday, 9-1 from Nov.- mid April. **The Domes at Mitchell Park**, 524 S. Layton Blvd.

Growing Power sells fresh produce daily from its warehouse, where it is grown there all year round at about 100 hoop style hot houses. These chemical free micro greens and vegetables will be among the freshest you will taste. They also team up with vendors Saturdays, 8-12 during winter. 5500 W. Silver Spring Dr. www.growingpower.org

FIREWORKS

Most people only get to see fireworks once a year on the 4th of July. Here in Milwaukee, there's a fireworks show nearly every weekend during summer. Fireworks are generally set off from the water near Summerfest grounds. We still do have the annual Independence Day fireworks, and each village within the county tends to have them on different days, so you could catch more than one show. For information statewide, you can use this website and enter your home location. It will show you the dates for fireworks, and in some cases they are rated as to the quality of the show..
www.fireworksinwisconsin.com

FISH

Approximately 15 of the county parks have lagoons, which are stocked with rainbow trout and yellow perch. Lake Michigan is stocked with Chinook salmon, so that parks on the river may have migrating salmon seasonally. Wisconsin fishing regulations apply, which means anyone age 16 and older needs a license. An inland trout stamp is also required to fish for or possess trout. Limits are posted near the bodies of water. No boats are allowed on the lagoons with the exception of vendor boats at Veteran's Park lagoon and Urban Ecology Center canoes at Washington Park. There are handicapped accessible decks at Washington Park, Veterans Park, Scout Lake, McKinley Park, and Milwaukee River Parkway.

Fishing charters are available on Lake Michigan through a variety of charter companies, which are all based at McKinley Marina. You can also fish off the pier at McKinley Marina, or the inlet near Lincoln Memorial Drive across from Collectivo at the Lake.

You can fish the river or lakefront at the following parks, and I've included a few tips from fishermen I've met at the parks:
Doctor's Park-jetties allow you further into the lake, but some may be

submerged after strong winds. Brown trout is best here.

Estabrook Park- trout, salmon, walleye, bass, steelhead and more in the river below the biergarten. You will also find stocked fish and even bright orange koi in the lagoon.

Kletzsch Park- fantastic angling at the falls. This can be quite crowded in fall.

Menomonee River, Miller Park area- salmon during fall. Other fish too when water is high.

Caesar's Park- prime spot for steelhead in the river here but there is a strong current.

Grant Park- near the Mill Pond on Oak Creek Parkway there's a small stream where you can fly fish.

South Shore Park/Yacht Club- pike, although casting can be difficult with so many boats.

Summerfest Grounds/Lakeshore State Park- fish at the mouth of the Milwaukee River in early morning for steelhead or Lake Michigan for brown trout.

When the ice is 6 inches thick, lagoons open for ice fishing at the following parks:

Brown Deer, 7835 N. Green Bay Rd.

Greenfield, 2028 S. 124 St.

Humboldt, 3000 S. Howell Ave.

McCarty, 2567 S. 79 St.

McGovern, 5400 N. 51 St.

Scout Lake, 5902 W. Loomis Rd.

Washington, 1859 N. 40 St.

Wilson, 1601 W. Howard Ave.

Be mindful of the skating areas and don't fish there. Usually the DNR holds an ice fishing event during winter to get children interested in the sport. They provide fishing equipment, and it's free. An adult must accompany children under 5. Call the DNR at (414)263-8614 for more information.

For up to date fishing reports, www.lake-link.com/wisconsin-fishing-reports/

FISH FRY

Who doesn't love a good fish fry on a Friday night? And the best part of eating fish fry in a park setting is that it's family friendly and you can walk off the meal afterwards.

The county parks hold fish fry specials from Memorial Day weekend through Labor Day Weekend at the clubhouses of 3 parks.

Brown Deer, 7835. N Green Bay Rd. (414)351-8220
Grant Park, 100 E. Hawthorn (414)762-4817
Whitnall Park, 5879 S. 92nd St. (414)525-4765

Dinners include cod with fries or parsley buttered potatoes, cole slaw, rye bread, and a cookie. You can dine in or carry out.

Hubbard Park Lodge also does fish fry on Fridays year round with live polka music! The menu includes cod, perch, shrimp, tilapia, and a variety of side dishes. There's a kids menu for 12 & under. Save room for dessert because the double chocolate cake, pecan pie, and key lime pie are very tasty! No reservations necessary. 3565 N. Morris Blvd., Shorewood (414)273-8300

FLOWERS

The best place for seasonal flower displays is at Boerner Botanical Gardens. They plant many and a wide variety, so there is something in bloom for the entire gardening season. Admission is required, except on several special days like mother's day or father's day when moms/dads respectively get in for free. 9400 Boerner Dr., Hales Corners (414)525-5601

Many of the county parks have plantings that are tended by friends of the parks, or by park employees. Others also have wildflowers. Probably the most scenic places for natural flowers at county parks would be Jacobus Park in spring, and Bender Park that has acres of meadows. Lakeshore State Park is also covered in fields of wildflowers that bloom late in the summer.

If you're looking for an indoor display, Mitchell Park Conservatory (The Domes) is a safe bet, and it's open for free on Mondays before 11 am, to Milwaukee county residents by showing a driver's license with a local address. 524 S. Layton Blvd. (414)257-7275 www.milwaukeedomes.org

FOLK DANCE

If you always wanted to be a folk dancer, Hart Park in Wauwatosa is the place for you on Tuesday nights. They call themselves Tuesday Night Folkdancers AKA International Dance-Milwaukee. For just a few dollars you can participate weekly. No dancing on the 2nd Tuesday of each month, but then it's on a Thursday. It doesn't matter what you know about folk dancing. All are welcome to try. 7300 W. Chestnut, Wauwatosa.

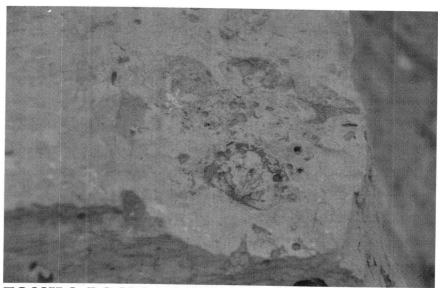

FOSSILS, ROCKS & MINERAL HUNTING

Milwaukee's topmost layer of bedrock is chock-full of fossils — remains of marine animals dating back to 443 million years ago when much of Wisconsin was covered in a shallow tropical sea, allowing reefs and early forms of life to flourish. If you stop at the Milwaukee Public Museum, you can see a pretty interesting depiction of what the reef that used to cover Milwaukee probably looked like.

Parts of Wisconsin were submerged during the Devonian Period, and today, evidence of this 416 to 360-million year old shallow inland sea can only be found in a narrow strip starting in northeastern Milwaukee and extending only as far north as Lake Church Road, a few miles above Port Washington.

And of this entire strip, only one site can be easily accessed — a blue-gray rocky outcrop in Whitefish Bay's **Estabrook Park**, just downstream of the "tiny falls" below the Biergarten. All or almost all other Devonian sites have been flooded or filled-in after quarries along the river and coast were closed. To find this, go down the stairs to the river. Follow the boardwalk to the left until it ends. From that point to the bridgeheads that remain from an older bridge, you'll find this rock. Look carefully and you're sure to find shells embedded in the rock face. These rocks have also been known to house diamonds from glacial activity, and a rare mineral that resembles hair like crystals, called millerite, although it is said the best finds are probably still under water.

Big Bay Park is an excellent fossil hunting site for amateur geologists and paleontologists who may not have the interest, tools or resources for hacking through rock. If you know your fossils, you can find Lingula, Discina, Orthis. Stropheodonta, Chonetes, and Spirifer- basically ferns and shell like creatures. www.thefossilhunter.weebly.com

There are two additional reefs in the area. **Schoonmaker Reef**, also known as the Wauwatosa Reef or Schoonmaker Quarry, is a 425 million year old fossilized reef in Wauwatosa. It was the first ancient reef described in North America. It was declared a national historic landmark in 1997.

Soldiers Home Reef, at the junction of Wood Ave. and General Mitchell Blvd, on the Clement J. Zablocki Veterans Affairs Medical Center Grounds. This reef is also a national historic landmark. These mounds give you an idea of what the ancient reefs looked like. You are encouraged to look, but not to take away any fossils found here.

UW Milwaukee has a very creative Department of Geosciences, and they have put together 4 different walking tours of the downtown area that show off a variety of regional stones that were used in buildings such as limestone, sandstone, granites, and travertine. It's called a *Virtual Tour of Downtown Milwaukee*. This is a fun way to see the sights and enjoy the outdoors while studying geology.
http://www4.uwm.edu/letsci/geosciences/trips_tours/urban_geo_new/

FUN RUN

Whether you're a seasoned athlete or just a beginner looking for a bit of exercise, there is an event for you. Runs take place in Milwaukee nearly every weekend, some even during the winter months. Many are fundraisers. Some are just designed to get participants messy. Mud run, glow run, color vibe, color run, Santa hustle, breast cancer run...the list goes on and on. There isn't one comprehensive website that lists every run, but you can see many on www.runningintheusa.com and you can put in Milwaukee for all races within 25 miles. Most races run through at least one park. There's also a very special fundraiser annually to raise funds specifically for the parks. It's called Run for the Parks and is sponsored by the Park People. www.parkpeoplemke.org

GARDEN

If you'd like to grow your own vegetables and flowers but don't have space, you can rent a plot in a community garden. There are many sources, and some are located in parks. The Victory Garden Initiative is kind of an umbrella organization for all garden installations. but are best known for their garden bed installations in neighborhoods, parks, and private residences. www.victorygardeninitiative.org

In Riverwest, there's an impressive community garden at Kilbourn Park. It was started in 2009, and has grown to 133 garden beds, each tended by an individual, family or organization in the neighborhood. The Water Works Department of Milwaukee owns the land, but Milwaukee Urban Gardens has the lease for this project. www.milwaukeeurbangardens.org

UW Milwaukee Extension office has many garden plots available. The gardening year runs from about May 1-late October. Contact them at (414)256-4600 www.milwaukee.uwex.edu

Alice's Garden, across from Johnson Park, has rental plots in their fenced garden area. This is also a great resource for classes, potlucks, and inspiration. 2136 N. 21st (414)687-0122 www.alicesgardenmilwaukee.com

The Urban Ecology Center at Riverside Park has community garden plots, teaches classes about composting, gardening, and has a plant swap. www.urbanecologycenter.org

GARDEN TOURS

During July, you'll see many local homes and gardens become open to the public for garden tours. For a nominal fee or donation, you get a map of the neighborhood and can look at how people have transformed grassy yards into refreshing havens using shrubbery, flowers, water features, and yard art. The homes change every year, but if you check your local news source in early July, you'll find one near you. www.jsonline.com

Boerner Botanical Gardens holds garden walks through their gardens every week all summer long. There is a cost, with those being led by Melinda Myers costing more. Each week is a different tour leader and a different topic or plant. Meet in the Education & Visitor Center Atrium, rain or shine. 9400 Boerner Drive, Hales Corners.
www.boernerbotanicalgardens.org

You can do docent led tours at Lynden Sculpture Garden, 2145 W. Brown Deer Rd. (414)446-8794, and the Rotary Centennial Arboretum, 1500 E. Park Pl. (414)964-8505

GEOCACHE

Whether you are new to geocaching or a pro, the best place for information about this fun activity is www.geocaching.com. Many of the Milwaukee parks have geocaches placed within their borders. The riverwalk also has a few. Sometimes the geocache can be a historical marker, a great view (like the one above), or even a box with a surprise in it. If you download a mobile geocaching program to your smart phone, you can stand in any place and it should show you what is nearby. You use a GPS and often some coded words or tips to help you find the cache. There is even a special Milwaukee neighborhood geocache tour, complete with a downloadable passport. This is great fun if you're looking for a multigenerational activity. I'll give you a hint that one of the geocaches is near the lakefront at Veteran's Park.
www.geocaching.com/adventures/geotours/visit-milwaukee

Havenwoods State Forest has geocaches too. If you complete the "Trek Through Time" geocaching adventure, you can earn a collectible wooden geotoken. Pick up a booklet and borrow a GPS at the nature center.

GOLF

Golfing is more affordable through the county park courses, and they have 15 you can choose from. Did you know Tiger Woods got his PGA tour career started at Brown Deer 's Tournament Course? They often run specials. The best way to get tee times and information about courses is to go to their website. www.milwaukeecountygolfcourses.com

Currie Park has an indoor heated golf driving range that is open during winter. Look for the large dome. 3535 N. Mayfair Rd, Wauwatosa (414)453-1742 www.curriegolfdome.com

For the more adventurous and fun loving golfer, there is nightglow golf. You golf at night with a ball that glows. Tees, flag sticks, and holes are also illuminated. It is offered at 3 courses from 8:30-10:30 pm during summer.
Lake 3233 E. Kenwood Blvd. (414)961-3206
Hansen, 9800 W. Underwood Creek Parkway (414)453-4454
Warnimont, 5400 S. Lake Dr., Cudahy (414)481-4730

HIKE

Hiking is available in all of the larger parks, but there are a few trails that are worth a mention because they have been designated National Recreation Trails. Here in Milwaukee, we currently have the East Bank Trail, Jacobus Park Nature Trail, Kohl Park Hiking Trail, and Seven Bridges Trail (Grant Park). These are all generally maintained by volunteers, so on occasion, I've had to jump over fallen trees, or move branches. There is also a risk of flooding in springtime. You can find these trails and others at www.traillink.com or www.americantrails.org

East Bank Trail is ¾ mile long and features local artwork. It runs along the east bank of the Milwaukee River and connects Riverside Park and Caesar Park. It has a paved surface, and is an ADA accessible walking trail that allows better access to the Milwaukee River. It's part of a larger loop of pedestrian and paved trails called the Beerline Loop that extends from Commerce St. to Locust St. on both sides of the river. You can access the beginning of the trail at the Rotary Centennial Arboretum at Riverside Park. Look for the big turtle sculpture and you'll know you're there.

Jacobus Park has a loop nearly a mile long that takes visitors through a woodland island. The park is home to more than 160 native plant species, of which a number are included on Wisconsin's threatened and endangered list. Gorgeous wildflowers bloom here in springtime. 6501 Hillside Ln.

Kohl Park Hiking Trail is a 270-acre park with 2 main trails that go through farmland, wetlands, a pine forest, orchards, and follow a neighborhood easement. This is a good place to see songbirds and waterfowl during migration periods. During periods of wet weather, expect some of the trails to be flooded. 7603 W. County Line Rd.

Seven Bridges Trail is in Grant Park and consists of many bridges that run through a wooded ravine. It's especially beautiful in spring when the trillium bloom, and during fall when the colors change. There's a creek that runs the length of the trail, making it scenic after a heavy rain. From the parking lot at the bridge trailhead, you can walk to the lake and access the beach. Enter Grant Park at South Lake Drive and Park Avenue. Travel about 1/8 mile. On your left (east) are parking spaces with a path leading to the Covered Bridge, the trail's main entrance. The trail is open during regular park hours.

The Oak Leaf Trail is the county's paved multi-use trail and is 114 miles long. Because it is multi-use, it does tend to get lots of traffic, so you have to be mindful when there are lots of bikes. This goes through so many parks that it's difficult to say where the best place is to hike. There has been a fun program, sponsored by the Park People, called the Oak Leaf Discovery Tour. You can get a passport and collect stamps or secret words at the parks along the trail. Once it's completed, you enter it into a drawing at the end of the summer season, where you can win fabulous prizes at a party to celebrate. It's been incredibly popular. www.parkpeople.org

There's a great book that you should have if you're an avid hiker. It has 20 day hikes near Milwaukee, *Best Easy Day Hikes: Milwaukee Guidebook*. The author is Kevin Revolinski (Falcon Publishing). You can preview the hikes at www.trails.com

The Milwaukee River Greenway is perhaps the most interesting piece of work. It combines 878 acres of trails and greenspace along the Milwaukee River within the city of Milwaukee and nearby suburbs. There are currently over 28 miles of hiking, biking, and water trails along 6 miles of the Milwaukee River. 12 public parks are linked together through proposed and existing public easements on private land. 70% of the land is owned by Milwaukee County Parks. www.milwaukeerivergreenway.org/greenway

Havenwoods State Forest has more than 6 miles of hiking trails. Some are open to bicycles, and some are accessible to people with disabilities and families with strollers. The outer trail all around the forest is 2.7 miles.

If you enjoy company when you hike, you can join a meetup group that meets at least once a week for a walk along the lakefront, but they also plan hikes, backpacking, and camping in many of the area parks and forests. They are very active and visit many different places to do a wide variety of hiking: Haunted hikes, Kettle Moraine Forest, overnight hikes, candlelight hikes, snowshoe hikes, and more. Each hike or event is often followed by a social activity like drinks or lunch somewhere. There are actually meetup groups for a variety of interests, but to find this one, go to the website and put in the search word hiking. www.meetup.com

Brian Russart, County Parks Natural Areas Coordinator and his crew of volunteers, including members of the Conservation Leadership Corps, created a number of hiking trails in the park's natural areas. The Park People's website has up to date lists complete with printable maps for each of the hiking trails. There were nearly 30 when I last checked. This is a fantastic resource for the hiker who wants a change of scenery. www.parkpeoplemke.org/hiking-trails-milwaukee-county-parks

Lake Park Friends group often has hikes with different nature themes, led by local experts (historical, trees, birds, wildflowers, etc.). You can check their calendar to see when they are held. www.lakeparkfriends.org

HISTORICAL MARKERS & LANDMARKS

Milwaukee County is loaded with historic places, and many of them have Wisconsin official markers that tell you a bit about that history. If you're a history buff, you can access the list of markers at the official website and make your way out to discover all of them in our parks, and other areas for that matter. www.preview.wisconsinhistory.org

There's even a blog about that! A woman made it her mission to find all 550 historical markers in the state and photograph them. It's quite an interesting story with lots of photos along the way. wisconsinhistoricalmarkers.blogspot.com

The Milwaukee County Historical Society maintains a website that lists every county historic landmark by village/town. Some of the landmarks are actual parks, such as Lake Park, Hubbard Park, and Riverside Park.. Other parks have landmarks, such as structures, inside of them. The whole process of determining what is worthy of landmark status must have been difficult, but they agreed on 94 properties over the past 30 years. There isn't really a huge perk to being a county landmark, other than education for anyone interested in Milwaukee county history. No money is given towards restoration or maintenance. It's meant as a public service, so go out and enjoy what they deem worthy of your visit. Many of them are quite picturesque by themselves, but they also make great places to use as gathering places for photos.

Here are some of my favorites:

The Schlitz Audubon Center used to be farmed by Dutch and German immigrants. Draft horses were bred and brewery horses were brought here to rest when the Uihlein family owned it. They also owned the Schlitz Brewing Company.

The Cudahy Depot served the Chicago and Northwestern Railway where many new immigrants would come to meet relatives already living in Milwaukee. It's now part of an area called Immigrant Park.

The Oak Creek Dam, just outside Grant Park, has one of the prettiest waterfalls and was the site of a gristmill and sawmill. You can see the millstones, lying nearby the falls, which are thought to be the oldest man-made items in South Milwaukee.

The Flushing Station, that houses Collectivo Coffee at the Lakefront's McKinley Marina Park, was home to a water pump that was once the largest in the world. You can learn more about it at the educational display in the back room while enjoying your coffee.

South Shore Park Pavilion was built using relief labor as part of the depression era programs.

Kilbourntown House in Estabrook Park is sometimes open to the public, and is an example of a house from the old Kilbourntown settlement.

The Civilian Conservation Corp(CCC) built the beautiful stone bridges in Whitnall Park during the early 1930s. The CCC had camps in Whitnall Park from 1933-1938, when federal work relief programs played a critical role in the development of Milwaukee county parks and the parkway system. The CCC also built the garden house at Boerner Botanical Gardens.

The headquarters for the Milwaukee County Historical Society is at Pere Marquette Park. Built in 1913, it used to be a bank and has some huge vaults. You can even walk inside of them. The interior of the building is all marble with ornate gold painting. It's quite an elegant place and is often rented out for weddings. Admission is $5. They have a library that houses local books and photos, as well as a genealogy collection for any research you might want to do on Milwaukee or your own family.
www.milwaukeehistory.net

HOLIDAY FUN

For every holiday, there is certainly something happening in at least one of the parks. Cathedral Square is at its best when it welcomes Santa and all the children for decorating trees and drinking hot chocolate. You can hunt for Easter eggs at North Point Lighthouse, among other places. For spooky hiking at Halloween, Wehr Nature Center is the place to be. Want a place to watch 4th of July Fireworks? Try the waterfront parks.

To find out about what's going on in Milwaukee, including the parks. Try these websites:
www.visitmilwaukee.org
www.county.milwaukee.gov/parks

HORSESHOES

Horseshoe pits are available at Humboldt Park, 3000 S. Howell Ave, and next to the Senior Center at Washington Park, 1859 N 40ᵗʰ St. You have to bring your own horseshoes. The pits are normally covered with a heavy tarpaper to prevent the sand from blowing away. Just remove that for play, and return it to the pit when you're done playing.

ICECANO FUN

These appear in the heart of winter along the lake Michigan coast and are frozen ice volcanoes, formed by crashing waves that freeze. They are different every year, and are spectacular. Although you might see them at any of the lakefront parks, I've seen the best icecanoes at the Schlitz Audubon Center. They do an educational piece about them in winter, so if you want to see if they are on the water, you can call in advance. My kids have had so much fun on these. You can climb inside some of them, or slide down them. Of course, there is often open water just beyond where these lie, so always supervise your kids when they are playing on them.
1111 E. Brown Deer Rd. (414)352-2880
www.sanc.org

ICE SKATE & PLAY HOCKEY

The county's primary outdoor ice rink is at Red Arrow Park when weather permits. Generally they open just before Christmas and close in early February. It's a refrigerated rink, so even if there are a few days when the sun might melt the ice, they can handle it. This has a Starbucks, lockers, warming area, and skates for rent. They also have a skate sharpening service while you wait. 920 N. Water St.

There are several outdoor rinks maintained by the county, city, and villages in Milwaukee County. Most of those are very weather dependent, and the ice may not be as fine if there has been snow. In most cases, you need to bring your own skates.

Wilson Ice Arena is open year round and is indoors. They sometimes have glow skating, and they offer skate rental and sharpening. 4001 S. 20th St. (414)281-6289

The Alyson Dudek International Ice Center, at Hales Corner Park, is supposed to open December 2013. It's a new outdoor ice rink, honoring the first Wisconsin athlete to medal in short track speed skating at the Olympic Winter games in Vancouver. The women's US short track speed skating team took home the bronze medal for the 3000m relay. The new rink would be Olympic sized and open to the public. It will be located behind the pool. 5675 S. New Berlin Rd., Hales Corners.

There's an outdoor rink for street hockey which is available for daytime play on a first come, first served basis from spring-November at Warnimont Park, 5400 S. Lake Dr., on the east side of S. Lake Dr.

The Sports Complex is available for rental for roller hockey, 6000 W. Ryan Road.

Ice Hockey can be played on any park lagoon where skating is permitted, in the hockey marked areas, when ice is present. These include Brown Deer, 7835 N. Green Bay Rd.
Humboldt, 3000 S. Howell Ave.
Lake Park, 2975 N. Lake Park Rd.
Scout Lake, 5902 W. Loomis Rd.
Sheridan, 4800 S. Lake Dr.

JOG, RUN, WALK FOR FITNESS

If you're a jogger or runner, whether seasoned or an amateur, you might check out www.runningintheusa.com

If you enter the city of Milwaukee, it gives a pretty comprehensive list of events in or near Milwaukee. Maybe this will inspire you to get your athletic shoes on and get out there! Many of the local runs start or end in the parks, so it's a good opportunity to see a bit more of the parks. Another comprehensive list with maps is available www.walkjogrun.net/running-routes/USA/WI/Milwaukee/

Wehr Nature Center has a weekly hiking group that meets Wednesday mornings at 1030 in the fireplace room for an hour long hike. Great idea if you like some company while getting in your exercise for the day.

A few suggestions for outdoor running routes- start from the War Memorial Center, on the corner of N. Prospect Ave. and E. Mason St. The most populated and scenic path is the paved Lakefront Trail that runs north from the Art Center along Lake Michigan. There's a great three-mile loop through Veteran's Park, which is just east of the south end of the paved Lakefront path. The park also has a 20-station exercise course. If you cross Lincoln Memorial Drive, just north of the Art Museum, you can pick up the Oak Leaf Trail, with 118 miles of trails through some of Milwaukee's most spectacular parks.

Just south of the Summerfest grounds, you'll find Lakeshore State Park, with paved trails that take you along the lake and connect to the river and the Hank Aaron Trail. The Hank Aaron Trail goes from Milwaukee's lakefront to the west end of the city. Start at Lakeshore State Park and end at Doyne Park. You can download a current map at the Hank Aaron Trail friends website. www.hankaaronstatetrail.org

Root River Parkway runs south from the duck pond of Greenfield Park, 2028 S. 124th St., through Whitnall Park, 5879 S. 92nd St., a nature preserve and a small lake. The loop is 12.6 miles one-way, so it's ideal for marathon trainers.

The Schlitz Audubon Center, 1111 E. Brown Deer Road, has 6 miles of trails through the 185 acres of land. www.sanc.org

Havenwoods State Forest has more than 6 miles of trails. The cross-country trail wraps around the forest and is 2.7 miles.

You might also check out the list of rails to trails at the Trail link website for Milwaukee. www.traillink.com/city/milwaukee-wi-trails.aspx. They give a photo, a small narrative, and then you can see the trail on a map.

If you enjoy running barefoot, you would think it would be a good idea to do it on the lakefront beaches. There are many who do, but I'd advise against it after a big storm washes up zebra mussels and stinking algae on the shoreline. Bradford Beach and Atwater Beaches are raked, but many others are not. Grant Park has a very long beach and would be a good spot to run. You can park at the bathhouse and go for miles on the beachfront. The most popular place for barefoot running seems to be along the Oak Leaf Trail, which runs the length of the county and is in all of the lakefront parks. Runners tend to run beside the trail, not on the trail, because it is asphalt or concrete.

The City of Milwaukee Health Department lists the distances around the park lagoons, for those who want a walk with a scenic view, like the one above at Kosciuszko Park lagoon. They also list malls with distances at their website. It's part of their campaign to get people more active. Not a bad idea at all! You can get a walking guide with tips on how to get started, as well as recommended exercises. http://city.milwaukee.gov/Walking-in-Parks-Malls.htm

Brown Deer Park, 7835 N. Green Bay Rd., Glendale (.45 miles)
Dineen Park, 6901 W. Vienna St. (.31 miles)
Greenfield Park, 2028 S. 123th St., West Allis (.57 miles)
Grobschmidt Park, 3751 W. College Ave., Franklin (.95 miles)
Humboldt Park, 3000 S. Howell Ave. (.34 miles)
Jackson Park, 3500 W. Forest Home Ave.(.55 miles)
Kosciuszko Park, 712 W. Becher St. (.30 miles)
McCarty Park, 8214 W. Cleveland Ave. (.45 miles)
Mitchell Park, 524 S. Layton Blvd. (.34 miles)
Saveland Park, 3700 S. 2nd St. (.11 miles)
Scout Lake, 5902 W. Loomis Rd., Greendale (.47 miles)
Veteran's Park, 1010 N. Lincoln Memorial Dr. (1.35 miles)
Washington Park, 1859 N. 40th St. (.78 miles)
Wilson Park, 1601 W. Howard Ave. (.61 miles)

KAYAK & CANOE

We have 3 different rivers on which to kayak and canoe, and they are part of the Milwaukee Urban Water Trail. The trail map was designed to help people find safe and legal access to the Milwaukee, Menomonee, and Kinnickinnic Rivers. It shows access points, portages, and resting sites, and also includes information on historic, cultural, ecological, or scenic points of interest along the way. The ultimate goal of a water trail is to connect more people to the rivers in their own backyards, and to inspire stewardship and protection of our waters. You'll find signage along the rivers to guide you, but it is best to download a map at www.mkeriverkeeper.org.

If you have your own kayak or canoe, you can paddle on the lake or rivers. If you want to use a rental, there are 3 vendors that currently rent kayaks and/or canoes. In addition, Bradford Beach is advertising that they will have sea kayaks available for rent in 2014, which will be a great addition for those who love a more challenging ride. (414)502-7368

Milwaukee Kayak Company is the latest newcomer and has a site on the Milwaukee River at 318 S. Water Street. The owner, Beth Handle, used to work with Laacke & Joys, a downtown business that had watercraft programs, which are no longer available. Paddling on the rivers downtown is a unique experience. You have the views of tall buildings, and access to restaurants where you can tie up your watercraft. You do have to watch out for debris in the water and passing boats. Opening times are weather dependent and seasonal. Rentals are in 4-hour increments, which is great because you can make a day of it and see most of the attractions in the rivers. They have both kayaks and canoes. Call (414)301-2240 for hours and prices.

Wheel Fun Rentals rents kayaks by the hour at the lagoon at Veteran's Park, 1400 N. Lincoln Memorial Dr. (414)232-5027. They are also seasonal and weather dependent. The lagoon isn't that large so you can easily see the whole area in an hour. The nicest thing about using their watercraft is that if you have people in your group who are uncomfortable with kayaking, they can go in a double kayak with you or opt for a pedal boat, also available for rent here. Everyone can have a good time.

You can become a member of the Urban Ecology Center and use kayaks & canoes for free at any one of their branches, once you've had a boat safety class. You can use their carts to take them to the nearby rivers, but it still takes 2 adults to properly launch and carry a kayak. They weigh about 70 pounds. Alternatively, you can transport the kayaks to another body of water on top of a vehicle, if you have the means. Urban Ecology Centers are located in Riverside Park at 1500 E. Park Pl., Washington Park at 1859 N. 40th St., and Menomonee Valley at 3700 W. Pierce St. The Washington Park Center has canoes you can take out on the lagoon at Washington Park. You can access phone numbers and maps at their website www.urbanecologycenter.org.

KITE FLYING

The best place to fly a kite is next to Lake Michigan, where there always seems to be a steady breeze. There are plenty of lakefront parks, but the one that is used most often for kite festivals is Veteran's Park. There are plenty of wide-open spaces, and if you show up with no kite, you can stop in at Gift of Wings, 1010 N. Lincoln Memorial Dr., which is right at the back of Veteran's Park.

There are 3 major kite events in Milwaukee. The Cool Fool Kite Festival is on New Year's Day from 11-5 pm. There is usually free hot chocolate and coffee. The Family Kite Festival is in May over Memorial Day weekend. Kite entertainers usually come from Illinois and perform with trick kites. It's quite a good show. The Fireworks Kite Festival is a fun fly on Independence Day weekend and all are welcome to participate before the fireworks. To find out about kite related events, you can go to www.giftofwings.com or call (414)425-8002.

LAWN BOWLING

Lake Park has a lawn bowling association, E. Newberry Blvd. and Lake Park Rd. The 2 greens there are among the finest in the Midwest. The season runs from May through September. The greens are open to bowling whenever weather permits. The club offers lessons to the public for $5 per person on Tuesday afternoons at 1 pm, and Wednesday evenings at 6:30 pm, June through August. Lessons are 30 minutes in length.
http:/milwaukeelawnbowls.com

LIGHTHOUSE TOURS

Milwaukee has 3 lighthouses; Milwaukee Pierhead Light, Milwaukee Breakwater Light, and historic North Point Lighthouse. Only North Point Lighthouse is open to the public currently, however, the Breakwater lighthouse was purchased by Optima Enrichment in 2013 and there are plans to renovate it and have it open to the public for special events, such as Doors Open Milwaukee, held every fall.

Located within Lake Park, North Point is a 74-foot historic lighthouse that is open to the public on weekends. It played an important role in the maritime trade for more than 120 years and was decommissioned in 1994. The lighthouse is attached to a 2 story Queen Anne style keeper's quarters. The inside of the house is now a museum that features a wide variety of artifacts about Milwaukee's famous lighthouse and its keepers. There are also exhibits about the heritage, culture and role that Milwaukee played in the regional maritime activities of the Great Lakes. The museum features a diverse collection of artwork, artifacts, documents, and educational materials. This house is settled on 2 acres of greenery in one of Milwaukee's oldest parks. 2650 N. Wahl Ave.
www.northpointlighthouse.org

MOVIES

You can find outdoor movies at many of the county parks during summer, and some of the local parks too. Most are free. Some have entertainment before the movie. Bring a blanket and come at dusk. The county lists their series called Family Flicks at www.county.milwaukee.gov . These movies are generally family friendly choices and are shown at 4 parks:

Veterans Park, 1010 N. Lincoln Memorial Dr.
Cudahy Park, E. Ramsey Ave., Cudahy
Humboldt Park, 3000 S. Howell Ave.
LaFollette Park, 9418 W. Washington St., West Allis

Point Fish Fry & A Flick at Discovery World is more adult oriented with R rated movies, and you can see their seasonal line-up at www.pointfishfryandaflick.com. These events include food trucks, Bartolottas fish fry, and adult beverages. They kindly ask that you do not bring your own food and drink.

There is also a Bike-in movies series at the swing park under Holton St. Bridge, near Trocadero on Water St. www.mkebke.com

MUSIC

The Biergarten at Estabrook has good old-fashioned polka music with accordions from late afternoon until early evening, while it is open during summer and fall.

Then there are the outdoor concerts, which are in abundance during summer. I think you might be able to find a park with a concert every night of every week. Sometimes you'll find a compiled list of all concerts done by OnMilwaukee, but otherwise look for listings at www.county.milwaukee.gov for the county concerts. If you happen to go to Washington Park, take a good look at that beautiful band shell from all sides. On the rear side, it lists composers that were important to Emil Blatz, the man who donated funds to have it built.

You can find additional information at each of the village websites, but here's a rundown of what usually is available.
Shorewood holds concerts along the river at Hubbard Park.
Greendale Park & Rec has weekend concerts at Greendale Gazebo in the business district.
Whitefish Bay Civic Foundation hosts ice cream socials with music at their Schoolhouse Park, and again downtown with a sort of block party.

Fox Point hosts Summer Serenade at Longacre Pavilion.

Wauwatosa has concerts at the Rotary Performance Pavilion.

Brown Deer conducts the Community Vibes Series at Brown Deer Village Park.

Oak Creek has programs at the Oak Creek Community Center.

West Allis has summer band concerts at Veteran's Memorial Park and music in the park at the Police Satellite station.

COA Youth and Family Centers hosts the Skyline Concert Series at Kadish Park.

Collectivo Coffee holds outdoor Florentine Opera and Latin Music at their locations in Riverwest, Bayview, and at the Lakefront.

Discovery World has Live at the Lakefront.

Bayshore Town Center in Glendale holds concerts in the Square.

During winter, the Domes host a winter music series, called Music Under Glass. From November through April, you can hear live music every Thursday night from 6:30-9:00 pm with regular admission. It's not only music, but sometimes there's a funky theme so you can dress up and have a little fun with it. Expect everything from polkas to jazz. The choices are incredibly varied.

NATURE CENTERS

There are several nature centers located in the parks. All of them host amphibians and nature displays that will teach you a little more about the local area. They also hold events that are family oriented. The trails surrounding all of the nature centers are great places to see wildlife such as deer, snakes, raccoons, opossum, rabbits, chipmunks, woodchucks, and a variety of birds.

Wehr Nature Center is in Whitnall Park. You have to pay $3 to park in their lot, but admission is free unless there's a special event. You don't really need an event to come here though. The trails are well marked, with easy access to the lake where you can find bullfrogs, geese, ducks, and all types of insects depending on the season. There's a wildlife viewing blind on the water. The outdoor patio has a nice sandbox area and playhouse. Kids will especially love this place. The friends of Wehr group is incredibly active and these 400 or so volunteers make the most amazing programs possible. Just to list a few: Winterfest, Owl Prowl, Halloween Haunts, Maple Sugar Days, Bat Night, and Cider Sunday. Everything I've ever attended here has been a lot of fun both for my kids and me. 9701 W. College Ave.

The Urban Ecology Centers are not for profit and placed in parks that do outreach to the neighborhoods where they exist. Their goal is to get people outdoors. There are a variety of activities going on at any time, and the best way to find out what you can do, is go to their website and find the event calendar. There is one website, but 3 centers.

Menomonee Valley has a slide that takes you from the entry floor to the lower floor where you'll find aquariums full of amphibians. You can see them being fed, and maybe have an opportunity to touch something like a snake. This center connects to the Valley Passage and 3 Bridges Park. 3700 W. Pierce St. (414)431-2940.

Washington Park is known for their Young Scientists Club afterschool program. You will find a variety of gardens- rain, butterfly, vegetable, and water gardens. You can take canoes out on the beautiful lagoon at Washington Park. 1859 N. 40th St. (414)344-5460.

Riverside Park has a secret entry via a slide in the outer wall that kids love. There's a climbing wall that is usually open on weekends. You can assist with animal feeding and see a variety of amphibians. This center connects to the newest park, Rotary Centennial Arboretum. 1500 E. Park Pl. (414)964-8505. www.urbanecologycenter.org

Schlitz Audubon Center is another not for profit center that teaches people to be stewards of our natural world. Located in the northern part of Milwaukee county on the lake shore, they have 185 acres of natural habitat, 6 miles of hiking trails, a 60 foot observation tower, and loads of programs. They are well known for their raptor program. There is an admission fee. 1111 E. Brown Deer Road (414)352-2880 www.sanc.org

Havenwoods State Forest has a nature center with planned activities and trained naturalists that can answer all your questions about plants and animals. You can pick up a trail map before heading out to the 6 miles of trails, 237 acres of grassland, woods, and wetlands in the city of Milwaukee. Indoors you will find live reptiles and amphibians. You can get a species list, geocaching adventure booklets, and many other publications. Borrow binoculars, field guides, GPS units, snowshoes and other exploring tools for use while you explore Havenwoods. Families with small children might enjoy taking Smokey the Bear for a hike, or borrowing a backpack with exploring tools and books. This is the only urban state forest in Wisconsin. 6141 N. Hopkins St. (414)527-0232 www.dnr.wi.gov/topic/parks/name/havenwoods

Hawthorn Glen is a 23-acre nature center that serves as a field trip location on weekdays for Milwaukee area school children. There are 5 different habitats interconnected by a trail system. The public is welcome to use the facility and the well-marked ¾ mile self guided nature trail in the evenings or on weekends. The nature museum is open weekdays 4-5 pm, weekends 11-11:45 am, and 3-4 pm. 1130 N. 60th St. (414)647-6050 www.milwaukeerecreation.net/hawthorn-glen

PARANORMAL ACTIVITY

I'm not a ghost hunter myself, but I know there are those who enjoy a fright now and then. There are at least 4 places that have been reported as haunted in our parks.

North Point Lighthouse, located at one of the oldest parks in the county, Lake Park. Reports of activity include hearing and seeing children, hearing laughter, cold spots, and an overall feeling of not being welcomed.

Also in Lake Park, the **Lion Bridges** have had reports of children standing by the lions.

Grant Park supposedly has a haunted **Seven Bridges Trail** where people say if you look off the main bridge towards the ravine, you can see sparkles.

Lastly, **Bender Park** in the southern part of the county where there used to be a number of houses that were demolished.

I can't say that I've experienced anything paranormal during my treks through the parks. Heed park closing times when visiting these parks, or you may be ticketed. www.milwaukeeparanormal.com

PARK FRIENDS

Many of the parks have friends groups, which meet to discuss park improvements, do fundraising, and schedule volunteer led events. They hold park cleanups and facilitate weed-out sessions to maintain high quality natural areas. Many create newsletters or inform the public about park issues. In general, they rally support to keep the parks beautiful and open for business. Without these friends groups, so many wonderful programs would not exist. If you're looking to meet community minded people like yourself, or have a suggestion about a specific park, this is the place to go. For a complete list of the approximately 50 Friends Groups along with contact information go to www.parkpeoplemke.org

PEDAL BOATS

You can rent pedal boats in 2 sizes at Veteran's Park lagoon 7 days a week during summer months, and on weekends during fall. They have a 2-passenger or a 4-passenger boat. You can rent by the hour and pedal the entire lagoon area. These include life vests. Wheel Fun Rentals 1400 N. Lincoln Memorial Dr. (414)232-5027

PHOTOGRAPHY

If you like nature photography, virtually any park may do. There's a camera club that meets at the Wehr Nature Center. They host events and have contests for best photos. www.wnccameraclub.com

If you have a photo shoot in mind, here are a few of my favorite places. Keep this in mind if you need to do a wedding, family gathering, or senior photos. The sun rises over Lake Michigan all year round. If you're interested in shooting some people on the beach at sunrise, you can go to any of the lakefront beaches very early in the morning. Some have old concrete breakwaters still in the water and those can be useful if you want to set up something further out in the water. You can access them from dry land and walk out to the end. f you want the sun behind you, shoot early in the day and you can use the bluff as the backdrop at Atwater Beach, Klode Park, Grant Park, and Doctor's Park. The stairs at Atwater Beach are nice because you can set up a larger group of people and because there aren't any trees, you won't get shade on the faces. Atwater also has some very colorful playground equipment at beach level that will make any shot jump out. It's also large enough that adults can sit in the dish swing, even 2 people at a time. There's a structure there that will also accommodate a group that kind of looks like a Christmas tree, and another that is tilted and circular. If you like the huge white rocks, Big Bay Park in Whitefish Bay is great. McKinley Park has some pretty rocks off shore too that add to the interest in a lake photo. My favorite park for rocks, water, bridges, and beautiful flowers, grass, etc. is Lakeshore State Park. It has everything you need for outdoor shots. If you come late in the day, the lighting is awesome as the setting sun reflects on the waterside of the park. When you want to use the city as a backdrop, there are 2 possible locations and they are both just off North Ave near Holton- Kadish Park with the pavilion, and on the other side and up higher is Kilbourn Reservoir. If there are puffy white clouds with a blue sky, this makes it even better.

For all around interest along the river, go to the river walk. You can get interesting buildings, structures, color...no matter what season. Don't forget the Bronze Fonz is there too. If you're willing to pay a little bit, you can visit Villa Terrace. That's a gorgeous old house with a pretty courtyard and grounds that usually have something in bloom, as well as an arch constructed of trees. Naturally, Boerner Botanic Gardens and Lynden Sculpture Gardens are great for outdoor shots with flowers, trees, and art. Grohmann Museum has a statue garden on their rooftop that would make some nice photos with sky and greenspace mixed up with bronze statues.

Don't forget the historic aspects of Milwaukee while you're at it. I believe the best photos of the Basilica of St. Josaphat are taken from across the pond at Kosciusko Park, when you can see the reflection in the water. Lake Park also has several interesting places you might like to photograph. It has a waterfall, lions bridge, wooded ravine, and of course the grand staircase. Trimborn Farm is full of historic farm buildings that are picturesque. And there's a cabin in Juneau Park that is in stark contrast to the high rise buildings behind it. Grant Park has the famous Covered Bridge head at Seven Bridges Trail.

Gazebos are in 5 county parks. Boerner Botanical Gardens has a classic wood and stone structure in the annual garden. Pere Marquette Park has a modern structure with a bronze roof. You have the riverwalk and river view just behind it. Washington Park has a gazebo in picnic area 3. Wilson Park has a classic wooden structure in picnic area 6a. Zeidler Union Square has a classic structure also. All of these are great when you want something a bit more formal like engagement or prom photos.

PICNIC

The picnic is still alive and well. Go to any park on a summer weekend and you'll find grills fired up, kids running around, and picnic tables full of good food. Normally you can just drop in at any park and bring your picnic basket, but if you have a larger group, or plan to have alcohol, you will need a picnic permit at the county parks from May 1-October 31. Costs depend on the number of people you expect to picnic with. If you want to bring a bounce house, you'll need to bring a generator and ensure you have insurance to cover injuries. Every county park has a map on the county parks website, and on them are shown picnic areas, so if you want to find the best place to find a table, check out the individual maps. www.county.milwaukee.gov

If you want to be spontaneous and need some sandwiches, I will highly recommend a Milwaukee legend, Koppa's Fulbeli Deli at 1940 N. Farwell. They self advertise their world's best sandwiches, and I haven't met anyone who didn't agree. This deli and grocery store is weird and wonderful with taxidermy in the aisles, interesting wall decorations, a free Atari game, and quite possibly every beverage ever known to man. It's an attraction you won't want to miss.

PLAYGROUNDS

Our parks have some of the newest and nicest playgrounds around. And the best thing is that they are not all the same. Be sure to check out multiple parks and find your favorite. Most of the replacement equipment comes along with the new foam padded surface underneath. There are separate tot lots in many of the parks for the younger kids. It would be impossible to list every playground in the area. Check out your local park and I'm sure you'll be pleased. During summer, the city of Milwaukee offers free supervised play at many of their playgrounds.

There are several very colorful and unique pocket parks at Washington Park that are nature themed. Most are climbing structures, so they are probably most appropriate for school age children. Go check them out, with or without kids, they are lots of fun!

There are 2 playgrounds that are wheelchair accessible, that I'm aware of. One is at the northeast corner of Washington Park. The other is at Will-o-way Grant Park. If you want a longer drive, check out Possibility Playground in Port Washington. It was built by volunteers on a bluff above the lake and is fully enclosed with play equipment for all abilities. www.possibilityplayground.org

Metroparent Magazine, which hosts Milwaukee Moms has a listing of park reviews that apply to the playgrounds as well as available facilities. www.metroparentmagazine.com/fastfindsandfun/parksandplaces/parks/

REMOTE CONTROL BOATS & PLANES

If you have your own remote control boat, you can sail it in any of the park lagoons. You probably want to wear some tall rubber boots in case you have to get wet to put in or retrieve it. Also look for tall grass and muck that could cause your boat to get stuck.

If you want to join others who enjoy building and sailing remote control boats, there's an enthusiastic group that sails at the Sheridan Park lagoon, the Wisconsin Scale Boating Association, a group for all ages. They promote the hobby overall from building to sailing. The fun about being at one of their events, is that you see an amazing array of different boats, depending on their personal interests. There are boats that speed at 60 mph and others that sail along. They come in all sizes, colors, and shapes. You can read their current newsletters and follow events on-line at www.wimodelboats.org.

The Milwaukee County remote control flying field is the place to be if you like to fly a model plane, or just enjoy watching. It's a field in 1000 acres of Root River floodplain purchased by the county. Obviously, if there has been a lot of rain and it's flooded, you won't be able to use the field. The field offers pit tables and ground pit space, and pilot station blocks following AMA Safety guidelines. To use the field as a pilot, you need to buy the required field license or membership, which is available at the website. 7000 W. Oakwood Rd, Franklin. www.ramsrcclub.com

RIVERWALK

Outside Magazine named Milwaukee one of the best river towns in the nation, and I have to agree. This area is a centerpiece of the downtown. You can walk the Milwaukee River Walk all year long. It's a 3-mile span that has 3 distinct sections: The Beerline Riverwalk to the north, the Downtown Riverwalk in the center, and the Third Ward Riverwalk to the south. The City of Milwaukee launched the Riverwalk initiative in 1988 to connect the Milwaukee River with business and leisure activities. It isn't yet up to ADA standards, which means it's a lot of work if you have a wheelchair or stroller, but they are making improvements every year. You'll find plenty of interesting artwork, places to eat and drink, and shopping. You can find lots of surprises here, including some hidden geocaches. At night this is a beautiful spot to take photos of the well-lit buildings and bridges. For a different viewpoint, take a boat ride or rent a kayak.

Where to start? I like to park near Pere Marquette Park because it's kind of central to the river walk and you get free Wi-Fi at that park, so if you're inclined to check in with yelp or tripadvisor, you can see where you can walk for attractions or lunch. There are also picnic tables and benches there with a nice view

If you are an art lover, you should focus on seeing the RiverSculpture exhibits, which number around 20. Some are permanent, and others come and go. They are concentrated between Juneau and Wisconsin avenues. Be sure to get your photo taken with the Bronze Fonz, located just south of Wells. Kids usually enjoy the tiles set into the concrete, which were done by area school kids. Gertie the duck and her babies are there too. For a current map of artwork with interactive photos, go to www.visitmilwaukee.org/riverwalk/artwalk

ROCK CLIMB

There is an outdoor climbing wall at the Riverside Urban Ecology Center, 1500 E. Park Place. (414)964-8505. For hours and fees, check their website. www.urbanecologycenter.org

There's also an artificial boulder, called Jake's Rock, for climbing at Hale's Corner's Park. It is a memorial to Jake Knapp, an 18-year-old avid climber who passed away back in March 2004 due to a sudden seizure. His family donated the money for this rock to be placed in the park. There are plenty of trees around, so the area is shady. Although the rock is synthetic material, it is unbelievably like bouldering on real rock. There are lots of pockets, edges, and jugs all over it. 5675 S. New Berlin Rd., Hales Corners.

ROCK SKIPPING

There's something so therapeutic about throwing rocks in the water and watching them splash. If you really want to perfect your skill at making them skip, go to the lake and practice. You need a day with little wind so the water surface is flat, and then a good supply of rocks. Three beaches come to mind when you need rocks. These are normally not the beaches that get raked.

Big Bay Park, 5000 N. Lake Dr., Whitefish Bay
Klode Park, 5900 N. Lake Dr., Whitefish Bay
Grant Park, 100 S. Hawthorne Ave.

Here are a few tips on rock skipping that I learned from a local expert. Look for a skinny, flat and round rock about the size of your palm, which is just heavy enough to withstand breezes, but light enough to throw. Put your index finger against the edge of the rock while holding the flat sides with your thumb on one side and middle finger on the other. Stand with your feet shoulder width apart facing sideways to the water. Then flick your rock across the surface with a sharp movement of the wrist. Keep trying and eventually you'll be an expert!

ROLLERBLADE

I hadn't been rollerblading in many years, so when I decided to try it out, a friend had a great idea. We could bring our kids along in strollers for extra balance. I have to admit, it was genius. I never fell and no one knew that I didn't really have a clue how to stop. At least the stroller had brakes! We called it stroller blading, and I'd encourage you to try it if you are a beginner and looking for an excuse to get more exercise in a beautiful setting. It's much faster than walking, and can be lots of fun.

There are primarily 2 trails used for rollerblading, the Oak Leaf Trail, and the Hank Aaron Trail. Both are paved in most spots, however there are still portions that are stone covered outside of the city center. I believe the most scenic route is along the lakefront, but it can be crowded at times.

If you don't have your own skates, that isn't a problem. Milwaukee Bike & Skate Rental at Veteran's Park has in-line skates with a full complement of protective gear for rent by the hour. 1500 N. Lincoln Memorial Drive, (414)273-1343 www.milwbikeskaterental.com

SAIL

If you like sailing, this is a great city to find a boat.

You can learn to sail with Milwaukee Community Sailing Center (MCSC). This is such a unique and wonderful resource. I continue to hear positive comments about the program, volunteers, and staff who make this place work. They have a fleet of 80 boats. Sailors in our area donated many. There are adult and youth courses at all levels. MCSC's nationally recognized "Prams in the Park" program introduces sailing and water safety to children at Juneau Park and Discovery World lagoons. Students learn water safety, rigging, sail theory, basic maneuvers and practice a capsize recovery drill under the watchful supervision of MCSC instructors. Open sailing is available 6 days a week and you can use the boats by becoming a members.

The MCSC also offers 2-hour sailboat rides for 1 to 4 passengers. These sailboat rides are always conducted with a Sailing Center instructor aboard. You have a choice- take the helm and steer or just sit back, relax and enjoy the scenery!

These sails are subject to prevailing weather conditions, instructor and fleet

availability. To schedule a sailboat ride, please contact the Sailing Center office by phone (414) 277-9094, or e-mail at info@sailingcenter.org at least 3 days in advance. Sailboat rides are not available on weekends due to the high volume of membership sailing activity.
www.sailingcenter.org

The Milwaukee Yacht Club is the oldest active yacht club on Lake Michigan, with 140 years of sailing excellence. They run a sailing school for all ages. There are adult and junior classes that run during summer, which include all aspects of sailing, including racing.
This is the place to go if you own a sailboat and need a parking space in the marina. 1700 N. Lincoln Memorial Dr. www.milwaukeeyc.com

There are also 2 charter sailing agencies. Sea Dog Sailing has a 38-foot yacht, the Quinn Marie. You can sign on as a guest or as a sailor.(414)687-3203
Adventure Charter Boats has the Mai Tai, which can accommodate 6 passengers. (414)339-5090 All are available at McKinley Marina.

If you have an interest in sailing a tall ship, there's always the Denis Sullivan at Discovery World. They have day sails, which allow you to be part of the crew for 2 hours as you sail on the lakefront.. Public sails are perfect for all ages. (414)765-8625. www.discoveryworld.org

SALMON RUN

Salmon have been stocked in Lake Michigan since the 1960s. Though reared in hatcheries, the salmon imprint on the area where they are stocked and return as adult fish in an attempt to spawn. The rivers are generally too warm and low in oxygen for the fish to spawn, so eggs are collected and sent to the state hatcheries to start the next generation.

This is a seasonal activity that can be fun even if you're not standing in the water with waders and a fly rod. In late October and November, you may start to see the salmon leave lake Michigan and start their journey up the rivers. You will know they are running when fisherman start to pack the rivers. Then you just need to find a dam where the salmon have a hard time jumping, and you will get quite a show. We found the best location to be Estabrook Park, 4400 Estabrook Parkway or Kletzsch Park. 6560 N. Milwaukee River Parkway. Stand near the falls at either location.

SAND SCULPTURES

Go to any of the lakeshore beaches and you'll find plenty of sand. Bring your own buckets and shovels, and you should be able to create the sand masterpiece of your dreams. This is great packing sand with just a little water added. Our favorite place to build in the sand is McKinley Beach because it's rarely crowded, so you can pack your favorite picnic foods and make a day of it. They also have a concession stand that stocks popsicles and snacks. My son loves the small playground, and of course, I love that it's so close to Collectivo so I can pick up a coffee while we're in the area.

Whitefish Bay's Cahill Park at Woodruff and Fairmount, seems to be the place where all old sand toys go when they are retired. There are plenty of buckets, trucks, and diggers. You can stop by anytime with no preparation, and know your kids will have plenty to keep them busy.

Every year at the Milwaukee Art Museum's Lakefront Festival of Art, they invite a guest sand sculptor to do an enormous sculpture. If you need a little inspiration, stop by and see it.

SCENIC VIEWS

There's a park that is a defunct water reservoir, appropriately called Kilbourn Reservoir Park. This 35-acre park is on land donated in the 1870s to the City of Milwaukee by Mayor Byron Kilbourn. The tanks were removed, but they left the hill behind. There are stairs up either side, or you can climb the path up from the back, which is more gradual. Once you're at the top, you can see most of the city's highest buildings, river, and even the lake. It's a very nice view. North Ave at Humboldt.

Upper Juneau Park is one of the best spots to see the lakefront, especially if the leaves are off the trees. Stand by the statue of Solomon Juneau. Kilbourn at Prospect.

The Schlitz Audubon Nature Center has a 60-foot observation tower you can climb for some panoramic views of the lakefront area. 1111 E. Brown Deer Rd.

Climb to the top of the hill at The Rock Sports Complex, 7900 Crystal Ridge Rd., in Franklin, where you can see for miles. The hill is used for skiing and gravity biking.

SCOOTERS & JET SKIS

Scooters are mopeds that are single rider only, per Wisconsin law. Rentals include unlimited mileage, helmets, and goggles. You must be 18 or older. Major credit cards are required, as well as a driver's license. Scooters have additional cargo boxes for storage.

Cream City Scooters (414)988-8800. McKinley Marina.

You can rent jet skis during summer at McKinley Marina from Hands-on Science. (414)803-3515

SCULPTURES

Milwaukee is probably not regarded as a great art city, yet we have sculptures scattered throughout the city, just like the one above in Atwater Beach Park, Shorewood. Unfortunately, there isn't a comprehensive art tour yet, but someone did a great job of inventorying them and listing them on a wiki page. If you truly love this kind of art, go to Wikipedia and look at the list, then you can click on the name to find the location, as well as information about the artist, and in most cases, when it was placed in that location. This is helpful too when you see something you like and want to know more about it. The wiki page also includes some photos.
http://en.wikipedia.org/wiki/List_of_public_art_in_Milwaukee

The Riverwalk has a program of its own, called RIVERSCULPTURE! It's an outdoor gallery with some temporary and some permanent sculptures. There are 20 currently on display. These sculptures can all be found between Juneau Ave. and Wisconsin Ave.

I first read about extraordinary Cass Street Park in "Oddball Wisconsin", a book about strange places one can visit in Wisconsin. It's more of a sculpture park, than a playground, but it does have swings, a set of play structures, basketball courts, and a couple of tennis courts. It's in the Brady Street Neighborhood, so it fits right in with the character of the neighborhood. I highly recommend stopping by and taking a look at these beautiful fiberglass structures that are so colorful and delightful. This is a park that was dedicated while John Norquist was mayor, and there's a plaque that says a time capsule was buried at the park opening, to be dug up in 2098. It's at the corner of Pleasant and Cass streets.

All of the artwork was done by Wisconsin artist Marina Lee. She received a Mayor's award for the work in this park, which was a revitalization effort. The school and the boys & girls club uses the playground, which are directly across the street. She has sculptures at another park on the 3000 block of N. Bremen in Riverwest, called Snails Crossing.

Not so much a park, as a defunct residence, you can also drive by and look through the fence at "The Witch's House" in Fox Point, the home of deceased artist, Mary Nohl. The Kohler foundation owns the home and most of her art, primarily concrete sculptures. 7328 N. Beach Dr., Fox Point If you like this kind of thing and want more, check out www.jmkac.org/index.php/wandering-wisconsin-maps. There are unique sculptures to see for free all over Wisconsin in unexpected places.

Lynden Sculpture Garden is the former home of Harry and Peg Bradley, at 2145 W. Brown Deer Rd. With more than 50 sculptures and 40 acres, it is a scenic wonderland. They plan lots of activities throughout the year, geared towards people of all ages. They even have days especially for dogs! The grounds are beautiful in all seasons. www.lyndensculpturegarden.org

SEGWAY TOUR

We get a lot of visitors and the most difficult to entertain seem to be the young adults. This is something that I tried with a group of 6 young adults, and they LOVED it! Tours vary in price depending on how long the tour will be. You rent your Segway through Milwaukee Bike & Skate, located in Veteran's Park, 1500 N. Lincoln Memorial Dr. (414)273-1343. Prices start at $49. For the fee, you get a lesson in how to ride the Segway, a helmet, and a group tour along the lakefront, or if you prefer a longer ride- up to Brady Street and Villa Terrace. The segways have a storage pouch on the handlebars for keys, cameras, and water bottles. Although I don't recommend you take photos during the tour while you're riding, there will be plenty of stops and photo opportunities.
www.milwaukeelakefrontsegway.com

SKATEBOARD

There is a self-made park on the old tennis courts at Estabrook near the Biergarten. It's filled with unique ramps, an assortment of rails, a pole jam, wedges, mini-ramp and Quick Crete throughout. You can even find a bathtub!

There are a couple of ramps at the north end of Kilbourn Reservoir Park that are used by skateboarders. And there's been some discussion about putting in a skate park at Humboldt Park. If it is approved and built, you will find it near the wading pool at the southwest corner of the park.

Oak Creek has a skate park with wooden structures at Abendschein Park, 1311 E. Drexel Ave., Oak Creek.

West Allis has plans for a skate park, but the initial bids came in much higher than the funds available. If it does get funding, it will be built at Radtke Park, 84th & National.

SLED

The county maintains sledding hills which can be used for toboggans, tubes, and sleds, when weather permits.

Brown Deer, 7835 N. Green Bay Rd.

Columbus, 7301 W. Courtland Ave.

Currie (lit at night), 3535 N. Mayfair Rd.

Greene, 4235 S. Lipton Ave.

Hales Corners, 5765 S. New Berlin Rd.

Humboldt (lit at night), 3000 S. Howell Ave.

LaFollette, 9418 W. Washington St.,

McCarty, 8214 W. Cleveland Ave.

McGovern, 5400 N. 51st St.

Pulaski (lit at night), 2677 S. 16th St.

Whitnall (lit at night), 5879 S. 92nd St.

There are additional parks that have hills, but they are not maintained or groomed:

Kletzsch Park, 6561 N. Milwaukee Parkway, Glendale

Hawthorn Glen, 1130 N. 60th St.

Maitland, 6001 S. 13th St.

Sheridan, 4800 S. Lake Dr.

Wilson Recreation, 4001 S. 20th St.

St. Mary's Hill , 2323 N. Lake Dr.

SNOWBOARD & SKI

The Rock Sports Complex makes snow using the same type of equipment used by the 2014 Winter Olympics. Snow guns cover the hill, which allow them to make a 3-4' base in about a week. They offer all types of downhill snow sports. You will find traditional ski and snowboard runs, but they will be adding more terrain features. There are 3 super terrain parks, according to your expertise such as novice, medium & expert terrains. You will also find 16 runs of family tubing with a magic carpet, which brings you back to the top for more efficient tubing fun. They have rental skis, boots, and snowboards.

7900 W. Crystal Ridge Dr., Franklin www.rockcomplex.com

SNOWSHOE & WINTER HIKE

Schlitz Audubon Center offers great trails for snowshoeing in winter. You have to pay a fee to enter. The nature center here has a roaring fire so you can pack your own lunch and thermos, and enjoy it indoors after an invigorating hike outdoors. 1111 E. Brown Deer Rd. (414)352-2880. www.sanc.org

The Urban Ecology Centers have trail access and snowshoes for loan. www.urbanecologycenter.org

Virtually any of the county parks are accessible for hiking and snowshoeing all winter long, provided you have your own equipment. The Oak Leaf trail and the lakefront paths are normally cleaned of snow in many places during winter, so they are not good for snowshoeing, but would be good for hiking.

Havenwoods State Forest offers 2 miles of flat trails for shared cross-country skiing and snowshoeing. You can borrow snowshoes from the nature center when it's open. 6141 N Hopkins St. (414)527-0232 The Kettle Moraine Forest isn't that far away either. For information about using these parks, go to www.dnr.wi.gov.

SPLASH PADS & WADING POOLS

When you want to take the kids somewhere to cool off, but don't need a pool, maybe a park splash pad or wading pool will do the trick. These are designed for kids aged 7 and under, with open times during summer for just a few hours every day. For the latest list of facilities you can check the county website under pools. Anyone not potty trained must wear swim diapers, and generally there are open restrooms for changing facilities.

My son and grandson love Gordon Park's splash pad and Humboldt Park's wading pool. Both have nice playgrounds right beside the water. At Humboldt Park, there's an ice pop vendor, so be sure to take some money with you, in case you're lucky enough to find him. They are $1.50 and come in about 6 different flavors. www.county.milwaukee.gov

Bayshore Town Center also has a splash pad with more extensive hours. It's closed during evening concerts. They offer a free towel service, courtesy of the Jewish Community Center. www.bayshoretowncenter.com

STAIR CLIMB

Forget the Stairmaster while the weather is nice. We have plenty of stairs in the parks that will do just fine on a nice day when you need an extra workout. Most of the stairs can be found along the beach parks that have a bluff. An added bonus is that the Oak Leaf Trail goes past or through many of these parks. And as a double bonus- all of these parks have spectacular sunrises over the lake or city, so if you're inclined to get up early, you may be rewarded with a nice view and cool breezes.

I'll start at the north of the county at Doctor's Park. If you walk past the playground to the restrooms and go to the far northeast of the upper bluff, you'll find stairs to the bottom. These are rustic. There is also a paved roadway, actually there are two that come from the parking lot at the north end. 1870 E. Fox Lane, Fox Point.

There are two in Whitefish Bay- Big Bay, 5000 N. Palisades Rd, and Klode Park, 5900 N. Lake Dr. Big Bay actually has a ramp that is paved, and a stairway that goes through the woods, which you can access at the beach level. Klode Park has a paved ramp, but there are also wooden steps. It's sometimes nice to have an alternative.

Lake Park has the double grand staircase that faces N. Lincoln Memorial Drive, at Ravine Road.

Atwater Park has a steep set of stairs, but there is also a paved ramp. I've heard it said, these are the most brutal. Lots of stairs in quick succession. Nice views though! E. Capitol Dr. at Lake Dr.

McKinley Beach- across the street from it actually. As you look west, you'll see a very straight set of steep stairs on the hill, but you can park on N. Lincoln Memorial Dr. at McKinley Beach Park and walk over. This is the link to Back Bay Park, 2315 E. Back Bay, so alternatively, you could start the stairs from the upper park.

Kilbourn Reservoir Park(above photo), on North Avenue at Bremen, is the highest park in the city of Milwaukee. The thing to do here, if you're feeling up to it, is to climb up from one side, do the loop at the top, and go down on the other side of the park. From at the top, you have maybe one of the best views of the high-rise buildings in Milwaukee. There are also plenty of benches, so if you tire, you can sit and enjoy the view.

STAND UP PADDLEBOARD (SUP)

This is a new sport for Milwaukee. If you have good balance, you can rent a paddleboard and an oar at Wheel Fun Rentals, located at the lagoon in front of Veteran's Park (1400 N. Lincoln Memorial Dr.) during the summer months and on weekends during early fall. Phone (414)232-5027. They also rent kayaks and pedal boats.

If you really have ambition, there's a power yoga group that often meets at Veteran's Park lagoon for yoga on the SUPs. Call Milwaukee Power Yoga at (414)731-1550 for information about meeting dates and times. The class is open to anyone at any level of yoga or paddle boarding for a fee per class.

Bradford Beach will also have paddleboards for rent beginning in 2014. (414)502-7368

Milwaukee Kayak Company has SUP rentals available Tuesday thru Sunday, which includes a paddle and life jacket for 4 hours on the Milwaukee River. You can make a reservation by e-mail or phone, however, you can just stop by to see what's available. 318 S. Water St. info@milwaukeekayak.com (414)301-2240

STATUE TOUR

Statues say a lot about the city and the people who have lived here. Often we have historical figures, soldiers, and even sports figures. Peter Wilt, a local blog writer, did an unofficial tally of statues in Milwaukee in 2011 and found more than 50. That is more than you'd probably expect for a city this size. Most have been here for quite some time. It's rare you see a new statue being erected. The ones we have in the parks are incredibly expensive to maintain. For example, the statue of Brigadier General Erastus B. Wolcott, in Lake Park was cleaned and waxed at a total cost of $100,000. The statue above of Thaddeus Kosciuszko cost $150,000 to refurbish, although it had 103 years of wear. You may really appreciate these monuments much more when you realize that someone cared enough to raise the funds to clean and repair such a historic statue, and it sure looks better once all the green is gone.

There's a self guided tour that includes a small number of them (both in/out of parks) at www.gpsmycity.com/tours/monuments-and-statues-tour-in-milwaukee-5691.html or you can download a smart phone app of **Milwaukee Map and Walks** for the Android, or **City Maps and Walks** in ITunes.

The Milwaukee County Historical Society lists these parks that have statues:
Robert Burns- Franklin Place Triangle
Leif, the Discoverer- Juneau Park
Pledge Allegiance- O'Donnell Park
Immigrant Mother- Cathedral Park
Pere Jacques Marquette- Pere Marquette Park
Solomon Juneau- Juneau Park
General Thaddeus Kosciuszko- Kosciuszko Park
Commerce/The Pewter Lady- Jackson Park
Casimer Pulaski- Pulaski Park, Cudahy
Goethe-Schiller- Washington Park
Patrick Cudahy- Sheridan Park
Reflecting Pool Statuary- Boerner Botanical Gardens, Whitnall Park
Garden Statuary- Boerner Botanical Gardens, Whitnall Park
Christian Wahl- Wahl Park
Erastus B. Wolcott- Lake Park.

STURGEON RELEASE

Riveredge Nature Center has been behind the annual sturgeon release program, called Sturgeon Fest, although the location has changed a few times over the years. The last time, it was held near Discovery World at Lakeshore State Park. For a $10 donation per fish, you can release a baby sturgeon into the water. The lines are generally long, and each person receives an ice cream pail with their purchased fish. Then if you like, they give you a certificate with a number that matches a tag on the fish, so you can track your sturgeon for life. They tend to live a very long time, sometimes as long as 125 years, which may be why they are called dinosaur fish. This is a family event with special children's activities, educational displays (like a life size sturgeon replica that is HUGE!), music, kites, and kayaks. www.riveredge.us

SUMMER CAMPS

Camp registration usually begins as early as February. There are plenty of outdoor options in the Milwaukee area parks, and for most, you can register on-line.

The Milwaukee zoo has day camps broken down by age groups. You can click on the child's age and it should tell you what is currently available with the number of slots still open. These courses are great for anyone who loves animals. You get to work with the trainers and veterinarians, and see animals up close in a way you normally wouldn't. If you like sea lions, the sea lion splash program teaches kids how to feed and work with the animals in a program that they present to the public.

The Schlitz Audubon Center has an online brochure. During the school year, they focus on preschoolers, but during the summer, there are courses for all school age groups. Most of the day camp sessions are only 3 hours in length. You get a discount if you are a member, so if you decide you want to have your children attend multiple sessions or have multiple family members participate, it may be worth your while to become a member. It's a great place for you to work out as well. I know parents who enjoy hiking while their kids are in camp, and you can always bring a good book and enjoy a bench down at the lake. This is a great introduction for kids to water, nature, and animals. They even have a collection of birds and reptiles that visit the camp sessions. www.sanc.org

The Urban Ecology Centers have 3 different locations so be sure to check the location for the summer camp you are interested in. Membership here also allows a discounted rate for the camps. The great thing about these camps is that they afford an opportunity for your kids to try things that you may not know how to do (like kayaking or water sports, rock climbing, etc.) or not have the equipment in your own family. Once you're a member you can check out equipment to use all year such as snowshoes, skates, bikes, or canoes. I LOVE that they even offer a parent's camp! Not all of us had the advantage of being campers as kids, so this is a great opportunity to learn how to do some fun outdoorsy stuff that we can show off to our friends and family. www.urbanecologycenter.org

Camp Wil-O-Way, run by Easter Seals, focuses on kids that otherwise might not be able to attend summer camp and works with their disabilities to make it a worthwhile outdoor experience. There are 2 different day camp locations, one in South Milwaukee at Grant Park. The other is in Wauwatosa at Underwood Park. www.county.milwaukee.gov

Nature in the Parks, which is a UW Extension program, hosts Adventure Summer Camp out of 3 Milwaukee county parks- Wehr Nature Center, Whitnall Park, and Scout Lake. They have an on-line brochure that gives more information about the courses. Here kids learn to fish, do some hiking, outdoor cooking, and nature projects. www.milwaukee.uwex.edu/youth/nature-in-the-parks/

Bike Kids Wisconsin offers summer biking programs, which include a variety of other activities- canoeing, rock climbing, horseback riding, visits to science museum, etc. This is awesome for parents who enjoy biking but need some help teaching their kids the rules of the road or want more confidence in their own skills- such as changing a flat tire. They even offer a family camp and an adaptive week for kids with special needs. Every day offers a new excursion by bike. www.bikekidswi.com

Milwaukee Recreation offers a wide range of enrichment opportunities for people of all abilities and has an aquatic program as well. This is run by Milwaukee Public Schools so prices will be lower for Milwaukee city residents, however they are open to anyone. They center weekly activities on a theme and include some interesting field trips to parks, water parks, nature centers, the zoo, and sporting events. www.milwaukeerecreation.net

Lynden Sculpture Gardens is focused on both art and nature. This is one of the few that offers gardening. for children aged 4-14. Discounts are available for members. www.lyndensculpturegarden.org

Lastly, don't forget to check the local villages where you live for their parks and recreation department programs. Many have summer day camps in their brochures and even allow on-line registration. Your local parks department can get you discounted tickets to places like Six Flags, and other attractions if you need some family time as well.

SUNRISE/SUNSET

If you don't mind getting up early, especially in summer, head to any of the lakefront parks for a spectacular sunrise. The sun naturally pops up in different places throughout the year, so it may take a few visits to anticipate its location. You may find you have the whole beach to yourself at this hour.

Sunsets are a little less showy in Milwaukee, but I've seen some good ones while standing at Lakeshore State Park, or near the front of the Milwaukee Art Museum. The sun sets over the city this way, and the reflected glow that happens just after sunset is gorgeous over the lake. I've also heard that if you get to the highest point in the city, it should be a better view. In this case, you could go to the top of Kilbourn Reservoir Park at sunset, or out to The Rock Complex, in Franklin.

SURF & KITEBOARD

Most people don't think of Lake Michigan as a great surfing destination, but there are some who enjoy the smaller waves and colder water. Sheboygan, just a little further north hosts a surfing event every year and has been called "The Malibu of the Midwest." Here in Milwaukee, I've been told that the best time to get good wave action is late spring and early summer, but the water is quite cold. You definitely need a wetsuit. Fall surfing brings somewhat warmer water temperatures.

If you want to try fresh water surfing, you might like Atwater Beach, E. Capitol at Lake Dr., Shorewood, or Big Bay Park, 5000 N. Lake Dr., Whitefish Bay. I've seen surfing videos from Grant Park Beach, 100 S. Hawthorne Ave, South Milwaukee, so I know it is also a good spot. You can access the beach right from the parking lot there, whereas you have to hike down the bluff at the northern beaches.

Now, if you've already mastered surfing, maybe the next step is kiteboarding. Kiteboarding is similar to wakeboarding or surfing, but with more freedom. You use a directional board, much like a surfboard, or a bidirectional kiteboard, similar to a wakeboard to surf in open water, without any power generating devices. You use a special traction kite to generate the pull needed to pull you over land, snow, or water and hold your edge. Kitesurfing allows you to surf in, over, and out of waves to boost huge air off the water pulling tricks and go upwind, much like windsurfing, all while using a kite. Exhilarating! There is a group you can contact for more information about when they meet and how to try this yourself, www.kiteboardmilwaukee.com.

If you're eager to try this yourself, lessons are available through Adventure Bicycle & Kiteboarding, LLC. You can call (414)520-1493 for more information. They provide all the gear you need for making it a good experience. Wind is needed and is often not consistent.

Windsurfing is also something you could do on Lake Michigan. When I've seen windsurfers, they were often at McKinley Beach or Bradford Beach.

SWIMMING POOLS

There are so many nice pools in Milwaukee. Most of the outdoor pools are open from Memorial Day until Labor Day. For updated information about hours, and rates, check www.county.milwaukee.gov and look for outdoor pools. Noyes, Pulaski, and Wilson offer Aquazumba.

Grobschmidt, 2600 16th Ave., (414)762-4919
Hales Corners, 5765 S. New Berlin Rd., (414)529-3622
Holler, 5151 S. 6th St., (414)481-7160
Jackson, 3500 W. Forest Home Ave., (414)384-2028
McCarty, 2567 S. 79th St., (414)384-2028
Sheridan, 4800 S. Lake Dr., (414)481-4731
Washington, 1859 N. 40th St., (414)344-5400
Wilson, 4001 S. 20th St., (414)281-4498
Fox Point Municipal Swimming Pool, 7100 N. Santa Monica Blvd.

There are 2 indoor county pools, which are open year round. Both have diving boards, locker rooms, and snacks for purchase. Children 7 and under must be with an adult. Swimming diapers are required for those not potty trained.
Noyes Pool, 8235 W. Good Hope Rd., (414)353-2433
Pulaski Pool, 2701 S. 16th St., (414)257-8098

Milwaukee Recreation has a complete aquatics program for all ages.
www.milwaukeerecreation.net/aquatics/

SWINGS

Lots of Milwaukee playgrounds have swings, but one is quite unusual and worth a visit no matter what the weather, because it's located underneath the Holton Street Bridge. The park was made by a group of volunteers from Beintween with donated materials from Home Depot, and then given to the city. It was made of tires and included a bench swing, traditional tire swings, and a trapeze. There was even a baby swing when I was there last. It has night lighting and a gravel surface. You can access it from Water Street, near Trocadero or by the pedestrian/bike bridge near Lakefront Brewery. As I write this, the swings have been removed for repair but I've heard they should return again in spring, although the materials and swings may be different.

Atwater Beach Park also has 2 very large disc swings, at the beach level that will fit kids and adults easily. You're never too old to swing!

TEAM SPORTS

There are plenty of choices when you want to join a team sport. Milwaukee has teams for so many different interests, and for all ages. Baseball, kickball, softball, football, rugby, cricket, soccer, lacrosse, and volleyball. You can even do boxing at the county community centers.

You can go to the Milwaukee county parks website, select a sport, and get details for any sport offered. If you want to use a field, unreserved fields are often available free of charge on a first come, first served basis. Contact the Organized Sports Office (414)257-8030 for more information. www.county.milwaukee.gov

Milwaukee United Cricket Club has a summer league in Milwaukee. They use the cricket ground at Lindsay Park. A new AstroTurf cricket pitch was installed at the Lindsay Park ground a few years back, the first in Milwaukee. 4360 N. 87th St. (414)257-8030 There are also cricket pitches at Meaux Park, 1903 Villard Ave., and Tippecanoe Park, 1411 E. Warnimont Ave. www.milwaukeecricket.com
Oak Creek also has a cricket league that plays at Abendschein Park, 1311 E. Drexel Ave., Oak Creek. www.cricclubs.com

Lacrosse and Soccer are played at Uihlein Soccer Park. 7101 W. Good Hope Rd.

Milwaukee Recreation puts out a seasonal guide for sports programs. Most run 6-8 weeks. www.milwaukeerecreation.net

The Rock Sports Complex is one of the top tier baseball and softball complexes in the nation, with 12-lighted pro spec fields, which are all Major League and Minor League replica fields. Rock League Baseball offers play from ages 8-55+ where they play competitively for league championships. 7900 W. Crystal Ridge Rd., Franklin (414)529-7676 www.rockcomplex.com/ball-parks/

If you need batting cages for practice, you can find them at The Rock Sports Complex, and Pumping Station Park, 1311 E. Chambers

There's an Ultimate Club, which has league and tournament play, as well as pickup games. This is a sport played with a flying disc that is kind of like football. You can see them play at Kinnickinnic Sports Center, or Hart Park in Wauwatosa. Visit their website for more information. www.milwaukeeultimateclub.com

The Milwaukee Polo Club plays matches at the polo grounds located on Highway VV (the extension of Silver Spring Dr.) just 2 miles east of Hwy 83 in North Lake and 3 miles west of Merton. www.milwaukeepolo.com

TENNIS & BASKETBALL COURTS

For a complete list of county operated tennis courts, go to www.county.milwaukee.gov and select tennis. Courts are unreserved during daylight, but the night lit courts need to be reserved. There is a reservation fee.

If you like playing tennis, but don't have a buddy, there's a national program called Tennis Round where you can look for courts in our area using zip code. Then register to play with someone at a specific court. It also gives a bit of information about the courts. You can see how many, if they are lighted, phone numbers, and complete addresses. It's especially helpful if you're new to town. www.tennisround.com

There are outdoor basketball courts in many of the county and village parks. You can use them during daylight hours on a first come first served basis, as long as they are not reserved. If you want to use a court that is lit at night, you should make a reservation at the park.

There are indoor basketball courts at 3 centers:
King Community Center, 1531 W. Vliet St. (414)344-5600
Kosciuszko Community Center, 2201 S. 7th St. (414)645-4624
Milwaukee County Sports Complex, 6000 W. Ryan Rd. (414)281-2694

THEATER

Optimist Theatre holds outdoor productions every summer at Kadish Park's new amphitheater, near the COA at 909 E. North Ave. Presentations are free and you don't need reservations. Seating is first come, first served. Lower terraces are for blanket seating. Upper terraces and areas to the side of the terraces may have lawn chairs. You have to bring your own blankets or chairs. www.optimisttheatre.org

There is also a fun summer program, Kidz Days, at the outdoor stage at the Marcus Center for Performing Arts. This stage is between the riverwalk and the urban forest. It has a variety of children's performers three times a week at 10 am, and is free. They usually run a schedule on their website closer to the summer. You don't need tickets. Just show up. 929 N. Water St. www.marcuscenter.org

If you'd like to put on your own little production, there's a stage in Lake Park at picnic area 3. If it's not being used for a musical event or other production, you can use it. We have had fun making our own movies here with the kids singing and dancing. Everyone wants to be a star!

TREASURE HUNT

With a metal detector, or even an iPhone with the metal detector app, you may be able to find historic treasures, change, and other interesting metal objects. People who do this frequently say that the best places for finding items are Atwater Beach and Bradford Beach, because people tend to gather there in bathing suits and probably drop things out of pockets. Typical items found in these areas by metal detector aficionados include a variety of coins, keys, and jewelry.

UNICYCLE

The bright young college students at Milwaukee School of Engineering(MSOE) had a great idea to use Red Arrow Park for their unicycling club during the months when it's too warm for ice-skating. It soon became popular with passersby who just wanted to try it out. Now they have sessions twice a week where anyone is welcome. They provide the gear and you just need to find the balance. Tuesday, 5-7 pm and Thursday, 12-2 pm. You even get a nice sticker for making the attempt!

UNUSUAL GARDENS

Villa Terrace Art Museum has a renaissance garden in the backyard. You'll notice the large staircase and expansive greenery through a wrought iron gate at N. Lincoln Memorial Dr. This beautiful garden was made to resemble a 16th century Tuscan landscape, with modifications to survive the Wisconsin climate. The museum and gardens are open year round, with an official garden opening on the first Sunday in June. Go see it for yourself and admire the Water stairway, which passes through the crabapple orchard and flowering shrubs. There are 2 secret gardens and a thicket, grassy spaces and benches, bordered with a variety of herbs, potted citrus trees, dwarf fruit trees and statues. I think you'll find it quite amazing. If you have time, stop in for one of their musical sessions at Café Sopra Mare on select Sundays year round. You can grab a pastry and coffee while listening to small ensembles or soloists. 1801 N. Prospect Ave. www.villaterracemuseum.org

The Grohmann Museum (MSOE) has the most incredible green rooftop garden, complete with flowerbeds, shrubbery, 12 huge bronze statues and a pretty good view. For a modest admission fee, you can see 3 floors of artwork about Men at Work, and then go to the top for the scenic view. Only open during the spring-fall season. This type of roof is said to save energy and reduce storm runoff. 1000 N. Broadway. www.msoe.edu

The Clock Shadow Building, at 130 W. Bruce St. in Walker's Point, is another fun place to visit with a rooftop that not only boasts edible gardening. They also teach cooking classes and have a seasonal farmer's market. It is 3000 square feet of urban green space, and you can read more about it at www.edibleskyline.blogspot.com The rooftop view includes the Hoan Bridge and lakefront. Very pretty! Be sure to check out the ice cream at Purple Door Ice Cream. These are not your traditional flavors. Some are flavored with coffee, chai, red peppers, and even pumpkin. You probably won't find chocolate or vanilla. There are also some interesting cheeses at Clock Shadow Creamery on the 1st floor too. Delicious! This is the first urban cheese maker in Milwaukee.

Alice's Garden, 2136 N. 21st St., is a large community garden with so much more. It's across from Johnsons Park, a historic area that played an important role in the Underground Railroad during the Civil War. The park was once part of a farm where a runaway slave was hidden. Her arrival inspired local abolitionists to organize the Underground Railroad and she became the first 'passenger.' Wisconsin became an abolition leader and ruled the federal fugitive slave act unconstitutional. They have an area at Alice's that is a typical slave garden, and a labyrinth that is planted with herbs, where you are encouraged to step away from everyday life, slow down, listen, receive guidance, and be inspired and healed. During summer, try a weekly open labyrinth walk, which is hosted by the minister-in-residence. www.alicesgardenmilwaukee.com

WATERFALLS

There are several waterfalls in the parks, depending on how liberally you use the term. Perhaps the most beautiful is at Whitnall Park, near the golf course. It is fed by a lake, and after a good rain, it is at its best. You can hike to it from Wehr Nature Center, or park nearby and walk just down the hill. 5879 S 92nd St.

There's another beautiful waterfall at the Mill Pond by the end of Grant Park, on the Oak Creek Parkway and Mill Road. This one has some interesting stone bridge arches, but you can't actually get down into the waterfall, although fishermen have been known to gather along the stream just past the falls during the salmon run.

The stones at Greenfield Park are the main feature at the waterfall. It's not huge, but scenic. This takes a bit of detective work to find, but it is marked on the park's map at the county website.

Lake Park has a more narrow, yet very scenic waterfall, in a shaded ravine. It is 30 feet high and is fed by runoff from the golf course. Again, if there's rain, it is going to run more than if we've had a dry spell. This fall was built in the 30s with lannon stone, but fell into disrepair, and was rebuilt in 2010 by Friends of Lake Park. It is similar to one that exists at Big Bay Park in Whitefish Bay, which no longer runs.

There's a lesser-known indoor waterfall at Mitchell Park Conservatory, (Milwaukee Domes) in the tropical dome, 524. S. Layton Blvd.

There are also a couple of falls that are wide, but perhaps less spectacular, on the Milwaukee River at Estabrook Park, 4400 Estabrook Parkway, and Kletzsch Park, 6560 N. Milwaukee River Parkway.
You can download a park map for any of these parks at www.milwaukee.gov.

WATER PARKS

Milwaukee has 4 aquatic centers/water parks. The difference between the pools and the water parks is the size and complexity of the water rides. At a water park, you may find bigger slides, tubes, and a lazy river. All the waterparks are heated pools with zero depth entry. There are water play stations for the younger set. They also have snack bars and tables with umbrellas so you can stay and enjoy lunch.

Cool Waters, 2028 S. 124th St. in Greenfield Park
David F. Schulz, 1301 W. Hampton in Lincoln Park
Pelican Cove, 2201 S. 7th St. in Kosciuszko Park
Tosa Pool, 1800 N. Swan, Wauwatosa at Hoyt Park

They are open only during the summer months. You can purchase a day pass or a season pass. You can save a few bucks if you have younger children and visit before noon.

WIFI

As I write this, there is free Wi-Fi at only 2 parks- Pere Marquette Park, 900 N. Plankinton, and Cathedral Square, Kilbourn Ave. & N. Jefferson, but there is discussion about making more parks more Wi-Fi friendly. Check back with www.openwifispots.com to find other free spots as they become available.

YOGA

If you've been inactive for a while, yoga is a great way to get back into a fitness routine. It's one of the fastest growing relaxation and flexibility techniques that develop strength of body as well as mind, and is doable at any fitness level. For all classes, it's recommended you wear comfortable clothing and bring your own yoga mat. There is a fee for all yoga classes.

Yoga in the Park is a program, led by Edie Starrett that runs year round in the community room at Lake Park, just beneath Lake Park Bistro. This is a beautiful way to start your day. You have the view of the sun rising over Lake Michigan as you wake up and stretch. Every Tuesday 7-8:15 am. 3133 E. Newberry Blvd.

Several senior centers in the parks offer yoga classes.
www.interfaithmilw.org
www.milwaukeerecreatioin.net/oasis/

All summer long, you can join an outdoor yoga class. Classes are held at Bradford Beach, Lake Park, Cathedral Square, and the square at Bayshore Town Center. "Yoga Rocks the Park" holds events, featuring a wide range of instructors, at Lake Park at the base of the Grand staircase. Check individual park websites for more information.

The Schlitz Audubon Center offers Hatha Yoga Classes. See their calendar for details on pricing and dates. Registration is required. (414)352-2880 www.sanc.org

ZOO

The original zoo was built in Washington Park, but back then it was called
West Park. In 1892 they started with 8 deer and an eagle. By 1906, there
were 75 animals. We've come a long way since then. Milwaukee County
has a world-class zoo with 2583 specimens on 200 acres, and it continues to
evolve. It is county owned and operated, but is supported by the
Zoological Society of Milwaukee County. There are the usual animals on
display, but they have recently added zip lines, and a ropes course. You
can enjoy a carousel, train ride, sky safari, petting zoo where you can feed
goats, camel rides, and animal shows including Oceans of Fun Seal & Sea
Lion Show. Get tasty ice cream at the dairy complex, or chase butterflies at
the butterfly garden. They hold summer camps, special holiday events like
Boo at the Zoo, and perhaps their most popular event, zoo a la carte. You
will have to pay for parking in addition to admission.
10001 W. Bluemound Rd. www.milwaukeezoo.org

ABOUT THE AUTHOR

Barbara Ali is a native of Illinois, but spent the bulk of her adult life traveling the world as she served a career with the US Air Force. She is an avid photographer, world traveler, adventurer, and mom. She and her husband Abdulhamid live in Milwaukee, Wisconsin, where they have a "yours, mine, and ours" family of 6 children. The youngest, Omar, is the only one currently living at home. He has Down syndrome and has been her inspiration in creating a life filled with fun. His love of the outdoors, along with his free spirit, spurred her to do and see more. Together they create new adventures every day. She writes about them at www.milwaukeeparks.blogspot.com. This is her first book.

Made in the USA
Charleston, SC
13 November 2015